SCHOLASTIC
Spelling™

Louisa Moats and Barbara Foorman

Welcome!

Hardcover ISBN 0-590-34468-4
Softcover ISBN 0-590-34464-1

2 3 4 5 6 7 8 9 10   09   03 02 01 00 99 98

Contents

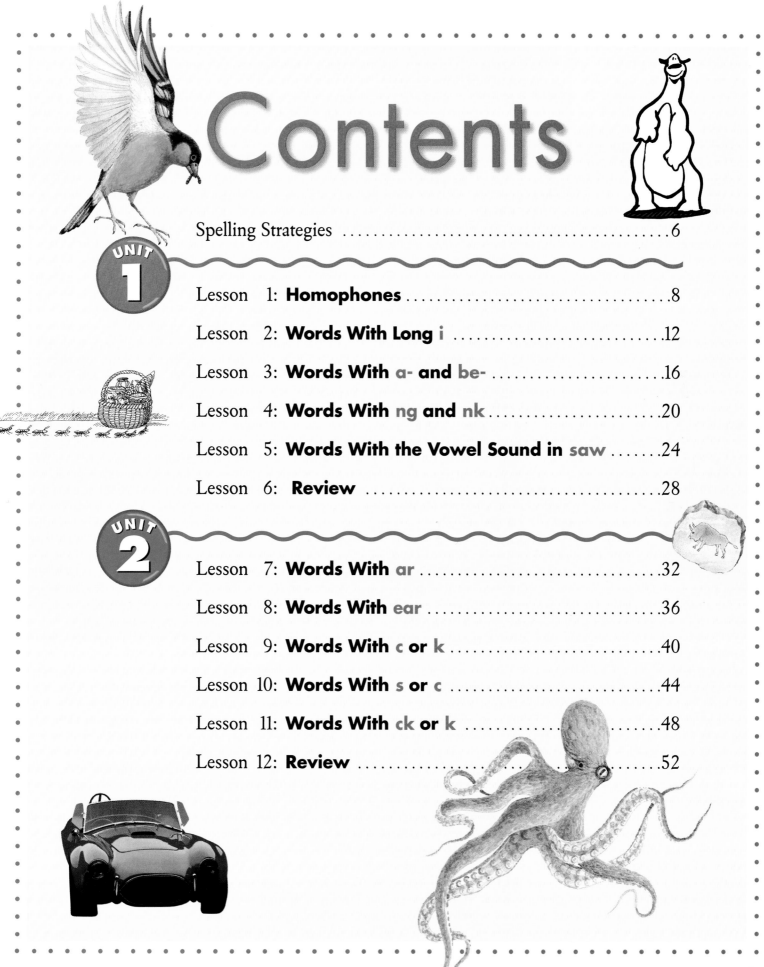

Contents

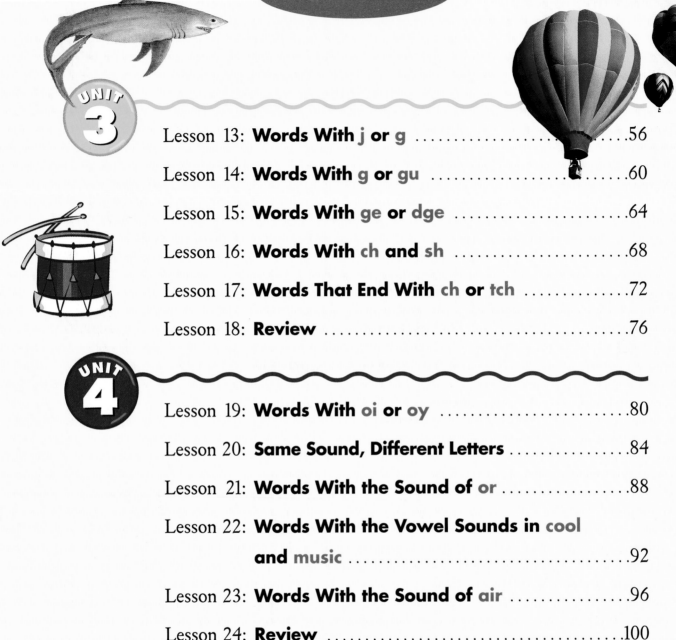

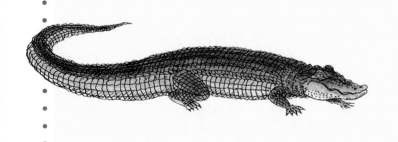

Contents

Spelling Strategies
Word Study Path

1. See the word.

See
Look at the letters in the word.

Say
Say each letter. Then say the word in syllables.

Link
Look for spelling patterns that you know.
Group the word with other words like it.

Write
Write the word until you remember how to
spell it. Say the letters as you write. Use the
word in a sentence.

Check
Check your spelling word list to see if you
spelled the word correctly. Keep your own
spelling journal.

4. Write.

Homophones

Ⓐ See and Say

The Spelling Concept

weak	right
week	write

Homophones are words that sound alike but have different meanings. They have different spellings, too.

> Eek! What a hard week!

MEMORY JOGGER

Ⓑ Link Sounds and Letters

Say each spelling word. Listen for the long vowel sound. Look at the letters that spell the sound. Then sort the spelling words on a chart like this one.

Word Sort

long a	long e	long i	long o

Ⓒ Write and Check

Which words in the riddle are homophones? Write the words.

_____

_____

RIDDLE

Why did Captain Navy rush to the store?

He wanted to buy a new sail on sale.

Spelling Words

main	right
mane	write
sail	side
sale	sighed
weak	road
week	rode
heal	rowed
heel	

LOOKOUT WORD

Review	Challenge
women	wade
brown	weighed
own	

My Words

_____

_____

_____

_____

Vocabulary Practice

A Build Vocabulary: Homophones

What's wrong with this sign? Someone wrote the wrong homophones! Write each underlined word. Then write the word that will make the sign correct.

Caps for (1) **Sail!**

This (3) weak only!
Great prices!
Come to the (5) mane floor
on the north
(7) sighed of the store.

Spell Chat
Turn to the person next to you. Challenge him or her to think of four more homophones.

(1) should be (2) .
(3) should be (4) .
(5) should be (6) .
(7) should be (8) .

B Word Study: Long Vowel Spellings

Read each word. Look at the spelling for the long vowel sound. Then write a rhyming word with the same spelling. Use the spelling words.

9. seal   11. code   13. toad   15. light
10. peel   12. towed   14. white

C Write

Use **road** and **rode** in a sentence.

_____

Spelling Words

main	right
mane	write
sail	side
sale	sighed
weak	road
week	rode
heal	rowed
heel	

Review	Challenge
women	wade
brown	weighed
own	

My Words

Spelling Words

main	right
mane	write
sail	side
sale	sighed
weak	road
week	rode
heal	rowed LOOKOUT WORD
heel	

Review	Challenge
women	wade
brown	weighed
own	

My Words

_____

_____

_____

_____

Quick Write

Choose a picture in a magazine and write a caption for it. Include a pair of homophones in your caption.

Ⓐ Write a Joke

You may wish to do this activity on a computer.

Many jokes and stories use homophones to make them funny. Write a joke or story you know that uses homophones, or make up your own. For example, *Why did Silly Simon take his worn out shoes to the doctor? He wanted the doctor to heal each heel!*

Spelling Tip
If you use a possessive pronoun, such as **its**, remember that it does not have **'s**.

Ⓑ Proofread

Here is Leo's funny story. Leo made three spelling errors, one punctuation error, and one error with a possessive pronoun. Correct the errors.

> The Lion and the Horse
> A lion and a horse met on the rode. The horse's brown main was braided with a red ribbon. The lion shook it's own mane and roared The frightened horse ran off. "I am king of the jungle," said the lion. "I have the main mane around here!"

PROOFREADING MARKS

∧	Add
⊙	Add a period
ℓ	Take out
◯↗	Move
≡	Capital letter
/	Small letter
¶	Indent paragraph

Now proofread your joke or funny story. Check spelling, punctuation, and possessive pronouns.

A Use the Dictionary: **Alphabetical Order**

A dictionary has thousands of words, but it's easy to find the one you want. That's because the words are listed in alphabetical order from **A** to **Z**.

Look at the first letter of each word. Then write the words in alphabetical order.

main _____

sale _____

heel _____

week _____

right _____

B Test Yourself

Match each clue to a spelling word.

1. lion's hair
2. most important
3. seven days
4. not strong
5. not wrong
6. to _____ a letter
7. part of a boat
8. at a low price
9. not top or bottom
10. let out a long breath
11. part of a foot
12. to get well
13. street
14. _____ on a bus
15. _____ a boat

For Tomorrow...
Get ready to share the homophones you discovered, and remember to study for your test!

Get Word Wise
The word **write** comes from an old English word, **wrītan**. It meant "to scratch." That's because the earliest writing was pictures scratched on stone.

Word Study Strategy

See the word

START

Say it slowly

Link sounds and letters

Write

Check

END

Words With Long i

A See and Say

Spelling Words

find	wild
kind	child
mind	children LOOKOUT WORD
wind	die
blind	lie
grind	pie
behind	tie
mild	

Review	Challenge
rowed	kindness
Friday	wilderness
milk	

My Words

_____

_____

_____

_____

The Spelling Concept

ind	kind
ild	child
ie	pie

The letter **i** usually has the long **i** sound in words that end **nd** or **ld**. The letters **ie** also stand for the long **i** sound in three-letter words.

B Link Sounds and Letters

Say each spelling word. Listen for the vowel sound. Then sort the words by the letters that include the long **i** sound. Use a target like this one.

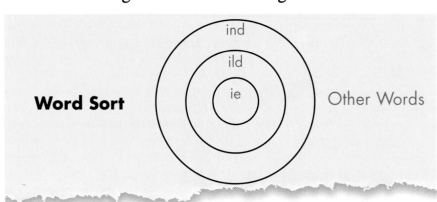

Word Sort

ind
ild
ie

Other Words

C Write and Check

Write the spelling words from the rhyme that have the long **i** sound.

_____

_____

_____

RHYME
Whenever Stuart's dad would eat berry pie, Some of it would always wind up on his tie.

I eat pie.

MEMORY JOGGER

Vocabulary Practice

A Build Vocabulary: **Opposites**

Some words such as **wild** and **tame** are opposites.
Write the spelling word that is the opposite of
each word below.

1. adults
2. mean
3. lose
4. live
5. ahead
6. unwind
7. spicy
8. sighted

Spell Chat

Turn to a partner and challenge him or
her to think of another pair of opposites
with long i. Hint: **dark** is the opposite
of a long i word.

B Word Study: **Beginning Consonants**

Read each silly sentence. Change the underlined
letter to make a spelling word that makes sense in
the sentence. Write the correct word.

9. The small <u>w</u>ild is two years old.
10. Legend says George Washington could not tell a <u>p</u>ie.
11. My uncle wears a bright purple <u>l</u>ie.
12. A mill is a place to <u>m</u>ind wheat and other grain.
13. Do you know how to bake a cherry <u>t</u>ie?
14. A lion is a <u>m</u>ild animal.
15. Do you <u>w</u>ind if I sit here?

C Write

Wind with a short **i** means "moving air." **Wind** with
a long **i** means "to wrap around." Write a sentence
with both words in it.

_____

_____

Be a Spelling Sleuth

Check out the weather page in
your local newspaper
each day this week.
Find words with
long i. Keep a list.

Spelling Words

find	wild
kind	child
mind	children
wind	die
blind	lie
grind	pie
behind	tie
mild	

Review	Challenge
rowed	kindness
Friday	wilderness
milk	

My Words

_____

_____

_____

_____

_____

Spelling Words

find   wild
kind   child
mind   children
wind   die
blind   lie
grind   pie
behind   tie
mild

Review	Challenge
rowed	kindness
Friday	wilderness
milk	

My Words

_____

_____

_____

_____

Quick Write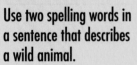
Use two spelling words in a sentence that describes a wild animal.

You may wish to write your story on a computer.

A Write a Description

Write about an imaginary animal. Include what it looks like and what it does. Use three spelling words.

B Proofread

Jane wrote this description of an imaginary animal. She made three spelling errors and one punctuation error. She also left out part of a sentence. Correct the errors.

Tip
Every sentence should have two parts—one that tells who and one that tells what happens.

> Slink is a wilde water creature who lives in the lake. Some children road past him once. They said he is purple and swims like a whale Has a head like an elephant! It's not a li to say he is as big as a bus.

Now proofread your description. Check for spelling, punctuation, and complete sentences.

PROOFREADING MARKS

∧ Add
⊙ Add a period
ℓ Take out
↻ Move
≡ Capital letter
/ Small letter
¶ Indent paragraph

Ⓐ Use the Dictionary: **Alphabetical Order**

There are many words in the dictionary that begin with the same letter. Words with the same first letter are alphabetized by their second letter.

Write the words in alphabetical order.

car _____

wind _____

blind _____

when _____

behind _____

bat _____

children _____

Ⓑ Test Yourself

Find the hidden spelling words. Then write them.

1. lieq
2. rubehindo
3. bechildrenz
4. tublinde
5. opien
6. okindit
7. smildor
8. tagrind
9. atien
10. newind
11. drchildz
12. ofindot
13. didie
14. rawildo
15. rimind

For Tomorrow...
Get ready to share the long i words you discovered, and remember to study for your test!

Get Word Wise
How do you **wind** up a toy? You turn a knob around and around. When you get ready to throw a baseball, you turn your arm around and around. That's called a "wind-up," too.

Word Study Strategy

See the word
START
Say it slowly
Link sounds and letters
Write
Check
END

Words With a- and be-

Ⓐ See and Say

Spelling Words

about	alone
above	along
across	become
again  LOOKOUT WORD	belong
ago	below
agree	beside
alike	between
alive	

Review	Challenge
children	beforehand
always	alongside
away	

My Words

___

___

___

___

The Spelling Concept

a	across	alike
be	become	beside

Many words have two syllables. Words that begin with **a-** or **be-** are often followed by a word or a group of letters you already know.

> Don't forget to put the a in again!

MEMORY JOGGER

Ⓑ Link Sounds and Letters

Say each spelling word. Listen for words that begin with a- or be-. Then sort the words on a chart like this one.

Word Sort

a-	be-

Ⓒ Write and Check

Write the spelling words in the joke.

___

___

___

JOKE

What's the difference between the chicken who went across the road and the chicken who stayed home?

about twenty feet

Ⓐ Build Vocabulary: **Synonyms**

Synonyms are words that mean the same thing, or almost the same thing. **Small** and **little** are synonyms. Write the spelling word that is a synonym for each clue.

1. similar	7. next to
2. past	8. living
3. under	9. once more
4. almost	10. over
5. by yourself	11. think the same
6. in the middle	

Spell Chat
Turn to a classmate. Ask him or her to think of another synonym pair with a- or be-. Hint: Try a synonym for "in back of."

Ⓑ Word Study: **Present-Tense Verbs**

A verb in the present tense must agree with its subject. Add **s** to each present-tense verb. Then write the verb that best completes each sentence.

agree   belong   become

12. My sister ____ to a drama club.
13. She puts on a costume and ____ a robot.
14. Everyone ____ she's great.

Ⓒ Write

Go from here to there. Write directions, using the words **across**, **along**, and **always**.

_____   _____

_____

Be a Spelling Sleuth
Look around your school. Keep your eyes open for words that begin with a- or be-. Keep a list of them.

Spelling Words

about	alone
above	along
across	become
again	belong
ago	below
agree	beside
alike	between
alive	

Review	Challenge
children	beforehand
always	alongside
away	

My Words

_____

_____

_____

_____

Spelling Words

about	alone
above	along
across	become
again *(LOOKOUT WORD)*	belong
ago	below
agree	beside
alike	between
alive	

Review	Challenge
children	beforehand
always	alongside
away	

My Words

_____

_____

_____

Quick Write

Use at least two spelling words in a question you might have about a special place you like to go.

A **Write a Travel Brochure**

Make a travel brochure for a place you know. First, list things you like about the place. Then, write a paragraph that will make readers want to go there, too. Use two spelling words. Remember to end statements with a period.

You may wish to do this activity on a computer.

Tip
Make sure each present-tense verb agrees with its subject.

B **Proofread**

Dina wrote a travel brochure about her favorite place. She made three spelling errors, one punctuation error, and one error in a present-tense verb. Correct them.

> Camp Out!
> Do you want to have a great time? Then you blong at Cedar Lake Camp. The day begins with a morning swim. Then you can ride horses accross the field At the end of the day, everyone sing beside the campfire. It's allways fun!

PROOFREADING MARKS

∧ Add
⊙ Add a period
ℓ Take out
↻ Move
≡ Capital letter
/ Small letter
¶ Indent paragraph

Now proofread your travel brochure. Check for spelling, punctuation, and the correct verb forms.

ⓐ Use the Dictionary: **Alphabetical Order**

In many dictionary words, the first two letters are the same. These words are alphabetized by their third letter. Write these words in alphabetical order.

beside _____

begin _____

below _____

between _____

become _____

Now check your work in the Spelling Dictionary at the back of the book.

ⓑ Test Yourself

Add **a-** or **be-** to make a spelling word. Write the word.

1. _ tween
2. _ lone
3. _ cross
4. _ live
5. _ gain
6. _ go
7. _ bove

8. _ gree
9. _ like
10. _ side
11. _ low
12. _ come
13. _ bout
14.–15. _ long

For Tomorrow...
Get ready to share the words with a- or be- you discovered, and remember to study for your test!

Word Study Strategy

See the word

START

Say it slowly

Link sounds and letters

Write

Check

END

Words With ng and nk

Ⓐ See and Say

Spelling Words

ring	finger **LOOKOUT WORD**
rang	wink
rung	drink
string	blink
strong	think
long	thank
spring	bunk
thing	

Review	Challenge
again	shrink
what	stranger
twins	

My Words

_____

_____

_____

_____

The Spelling Concept

ng	strong	string
nk	wink	blink

Some consonant sounds are spelled with more than one letter. The last sound in **strong** and **string** is spelled **ng**. The last sound in **wink** and **blink** is spelled **nk**.

Ⓑ Link Sounds and Letters

Say each spelling word and listen for /ng/ or /nk/. Look at the letters that are used to spell each sound. Then sort the spelling words on a chart like this one.

> Remember the ring on your finger.
>
> MEMORY JOGGER

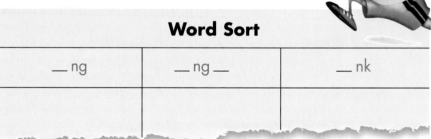

Word Sort

— ng	— ng —	— nk

Ⓒ Write and Check

Which words in the verse end like **spring**? Write the ones that are spelling words.

_____

_____

_____

RHYME
Bing made a ring
Out of string,
To remind him to think
Of an important
thing.

A Build Vocabulary: **Rhymes**

When words have the same ending sounds, such as **bank** and **tank**, they rhyme. Write the spelling word or words that rhyme with each word.

1. sang
2. dunk
3. linger
4. sank
5–6. wrong
7–10. sink

B Word Study: **Plurals**

To make most words plural, just add **s**, as in **springs**. Make these words plural.

11. one string, six ___ on a guitar
12. one ring, three ___ in a circus
13. one drink, eight ___ of water a day
14. one rung, five ___ on a ladder
15. one wink, forty ___ in a short nap

C Write

Use these spelling words to write a question.

spring   thing   think   what

_____

_____

_____

Be a Spelling Sleuth
Look for words with ng and nk in comics and cartoons. Make a list of them.

Spell Chat
Turn to the person next to you. Challenge him or her to use a spelling word to make up a rhyming phrase, such as a long song.

Spelling Words

ring	finger
rang	wink
rung	drink
string	blink
strong	think
long	thank
spring	bunk
thing	

Review	Challenge
again	shrink
what	stranger
twins	

My Words

_____

_____

_____

Spelling Words

ring	finger
rang	wink
rung	drink
string	blink
strong	think
long	thank
spring	bunk
thing	

Review	Challenge
again	shrink
what	stranger
twins	

My Words

Quick Write

Use two spelling words to write what you might ask a clerk in a craft store.

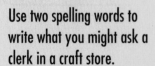

A Write a Conversation

You may wish to do this activity on a computer.

Make up a brief conversation between two friends. Imagine they're making plans for the weekend. What might each one say? Include at least three spelling words. Remember to use a question mark at the end of a question.

B Proofread

Sam wrote a conversation between two friends. He made three spelling errors, one punctuation error, and one error with a plural. Correct the errors.

Tip
You can make most nouns plural by adding **s**.

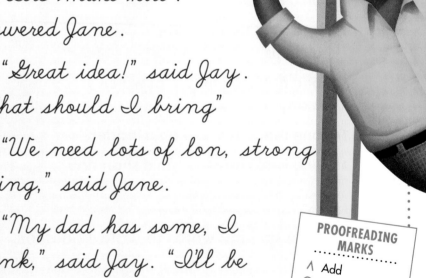

"Wat should we do today?" asked Jay.

"Let's make kite !" answered Jane.

"Great idea!" said Jay. "What should I bring"

"We need lots of lon, strong string," said Jane.

"My dad has some, I think," said Jay. "I'll be over in a wingk."

PROOFREADING MARKS

∧ Add
⊙ Add a period
ℓ Take out
↻ Move
≡ Capital letter
／ Small letter
¢ Indent paragraph

Now proofread the conversation you wrote. Check for spelling, punctuation, and plural nouns.

A Use the Dictionary: **Guide Words**

Guide words appear at the top of each page in the dictionary. The word on the left is the first word on the page. The word on the right is the last word. All the entries on the page are in alphabetical order between the two guide words.

> **thing • thorny**
>
> **thing** /thing/ *noun*
>   An object, idea, or event.

Write the spelling word that would be on the same page as each pair of guide words below. Check your work in the Spelling Dictionary.

spring   long   bunk   ring

blink • can't _____   lawn • march_____

spend • store_____   rather • rung_____

B Test Yourself

Add the correct letters to make a spelling word. Write each spelling word only once.

nk   ng   nger

1. ru __	5. stro __	9. tha __	13. ra __
2. thi __	6. spri __	10. ri __	14. fi __
3. stri __	7. wi __	11. thi __	15. bli __
4. lo __	8. bu __	12. dri __	

For Tomorrow...
Get ready to share the ng and nk words you discovered, and remember to study for your test!

Word Study Strategy

See the word

START

Say it slowly

Link sounds and letters

Write

Check

END

Words With the Vowel Sound in *saw*

A See and Say

Spelling Words

saw	awful
paw	aunt **LOOKOUT WORD**
draw	haul
straw	fault
dawn	because
lawn	water
yawn	wash
crawl	

Review	Challenge
finger	autumn
wishes	exhausted
walk	

My Words

_____

_____

_____

The Spelling Concept

saw   fault   wash

The letters **aw, au,** and **a** can stand for the vowel sound in **saw.**

Do you have an aunt?

MEMORY JOGGER

B Link Sounds and Letters

Dawn likes words with **aw**. Paul likes words with **au**. Say each spelling word and write it on a chart like this one.

Word Sort

Dawn's words	Paul's words	Other Words

C Write and Check

The chore list lost some of its letters. Fix the list. Write the spelling words.

_____

_____

_____

_____

_____

FARM CHORES

1. Get up at d__n.
2. H__l str__ to the barn.
3. Do the w_sh.
4. S__ the wood.
5. Y__n and cr__l into bed!

A Build Vocabulary: **Nouns and Verbs**

Complete each pair of sentences with a spelling word. The word will be a noun in the first sentence and a verb in the second sentence.

1. Sam used a ___ to cut the wood.
   Sam ___ a bird in the nest.

2. Hang the ___ on the line to dry.
   Jan can ___ the pup in the tub.

3. We got up at ___ to see the sun rise.
   When did it ___ on you that you had won?

4. Would you like a drink of ___ ?
   Use the hose to ___ the garden.

Spell Chat

Challenge the person next to you to think of three words with **au**. Hint: Think **autos**.

B Word Study: **Word Meaning**

Write the spelling word that goes with each clue.

5. move very slowly
6. make a picture
7. a grassy place
8. dried stems of wheat
9. terrible
10. you do it when you're tired

11. a cat's foot
12. for a reason
13. mistake
14. a cousin's mom
15. carry

Spelling Words	
saw	awful
paw	aunt
draw	haul
straw	fault
dawn	because
lawn	water
yawn	wash
crawl	

Review	Challenge
finger	autumn
wishes	exhausted
walk	

My Words

_____

_____

_____

_____

C Write

Use the spelling words **saw, water,** and **crawl** in a sentence.

_____

_____

Spelling Words

saw	awful
paw	aunt 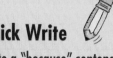 LOOKOUT WORD
draw	haul
straw	fault
dawn	because
lawn	water
yawn	wash
crawl	

Review	Challenge
finger	autumn
wishes	exhausted
walk	

My Words

Quick Write

Write a "because" sentence that explains something about you or your pet. Use three or more spelling words.

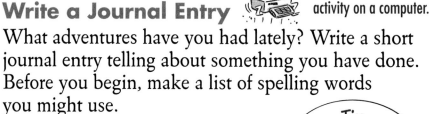 You may wish to do this activity on a computer.

A **Write a Journal Entry**

What adventures have you had lately? Write a short journal entry telling about something you have done. Before you begin, make a list of spelling words you might use.

> **Tip**
> Remember to capitalize the pronoun I.

B **Proofread**

Paul wrote a journal entry. He made three spelling errors, a punctuation error, and a capitalization error. Correct the errors.

> Mom, Aunt Paula, and I went to the state park for the day. Mom taught me how to swim the crawl. Aunt Paula cheered and cheered When i started to yawn, we went home. I was so tired I could hardly wauk, but I knew how to do the crawl.

PROOFREADING MARKS

∧ Add
⊙ Add a period
ℓ Take out
⟲ Move
≡ Capital letter
/ Small letter
¶ Indent paragraph

Now proofread your journal entry. Check for spelling, punctuation, and capitalization.

26 Lesson 5

Ⓐ Use the Dictionary: **Entry Word**

Read the dictionary entry. Look at all the different parts.

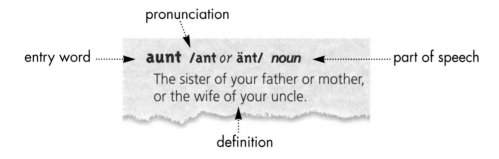

pronunciation

entry word ....→ **aunt** /ant *or* änt/ *noun* ←........... part of speech
The sister of your father or mother,
or the wife of your uncle.

definition

Write the entry word. _____

Write the pronunciations for the word. _____

Write the part of speech. _____

Read the definition. Write a sentence, using **aunt**.

_____

Ⓑ Test Yourself

Read the dictionary pronunciations. Write the
spelling words.

1. /ô fəl/	6. /krôl/	11. /wôsh/
2. /wô tər/	7. /ant/	12. /fôlt/
3. /lôn/	8. /dôn/	13. /sô/
4. /drô/	9. /pô/	14. /hôl/
5. /bi kôz/	10. /yôn/	15. /strô/

For Tomorrow...
Get ready to share the
aw and au words you
discovered, and remember
to study for your test!

Get Word Wise
Crawl and **crab** share the same
root: **krab-**. Think about how a
crab moves. Think about what it
is like to crawl on your hands
and knees. It makes sense that
the two words
are related.

Word Study Strategy

See the word

START

Say
it slowly

Link
sounds
and
letters

Write

Check

END

The Spider and the Turtle

An African Folk Tale

Complete each sentence with a word from the box.

| across | ring | thank | kind | wash |

Spider asked Turtle to dinner. "Oh, (1) you. You are so (2) ," said Turtle. "Your feet are very dusty," Spider said. "There is a river (3) the way. You can (4) your feet while I make dinner. When it's ready, I'll (5) this bell."

| again | crawl | drink | saw | sighed |

Turtle washed his feet and had a (6) of water. Then he heard the bell. He began to (7) back to Spider's house. When Spider (8) Turtle's feet, he said, "Your feet are still dusty! Please wash them (9) ." Off hungry Turtle went. When Turtle got back, all the food was gone. "What a good meal that was," said Spider. Turtle (10) and set off for home.

| because | below | beside | water | road |

Some days later, Spider was walking down the (11) . He met Turtle. Turtle invited Spider for lunch. "Follow me," said Turtle, as he swam to the bottom of the lake. Spider jumped in. He floated (12) he was so light. Clever Spider filled his coat pockets with stones. When he jumped into the (13) , he sank down to Turtle's home (14) . Spider sat (15) Turtle.

"Oh, dear," said Turtle, "We never eat with our coats on." So Spider took off his coat. Up he popped to the lake's surface! Turtle smiled and said, "One good meal deserves another!"

Meaning Clues

Write the word that goes with each clue.

1. If you can lift something heavy, you're _____ .

2. If it's the truth, it's not a _____ .

3. If you make a picture, you may _____ it.

4. If it's apple or peach, it could be a _____ .

5. If someone is in front of you, you're _____ .

6. If you're nice, you are also _____ .

lie

behind

kind

pie

strong

draw

Riddles

wash

ring

string

straw

yawn

Write the word that answers each riddle.

7. What did the phone say to the doorbell?

Give me a _____ .

8. What kind of berry can you use to drink juice?

a _____ berry

9. What might you do at dawn and at sunset?

_____

10. What did the cord say to the kite?

I like to _____ along with you.

11. Where do the soap and water meet?

in the _____

What's the Word?

Find each letter. Then put the letters together.

It's in **sat** and **sew**. ____

It's in **pear** and **pick**. ____

It's in **for** and **car**. ____

It's in **his** and **pig**. ____

It's in **bean** and **moon**. ____

It's in **get** and **ago**. ____

What's the word?

_ _ _ _ _ _ _

agree
thank
between
bunk
child
children
find
finger

mind
long
pie
right
sale
thing
week
wild

Advertise It

Write an ad for each product or place below. Make it catchy! Use at least two spelling words in each ad.

1. Crispy Crunchy Cereal

_____

2. Children's Science Museum

_____

3. Grandpa's Bake Shop

_____

4. Bright's Toy Store

_____

5. Joy's Department Store

_____

Tip
Remember to begin each sentence with a capital letter.

Look back at My Words and the words you misspelled in your Unit 1 Posttests. Use them in another ad.

6. Ford's Family Theater

_____

_____

Rate It

Write a consumer report about one of the products or places above. Use three spelling words to tell how you feel about it. Give it a rating from four stars to no stars. Proofread your report for spelling, capitalization, and punctuation. Then share it with your classmates.

_____

_____

_____

PROOFREADING MARKS

∧ Add
⊙ Add a period
ℓ Take out
⟲∧ Move
☰ Capital letter
/ Small letter
¶ Indent paragraph

Write It Right!

Read each set of sentences. Write the right homophone.

main   mane

1. We saw a lion with a thick, yellow _____.

2. He is the _____ star at Lion Country Park.

side   sighed

3. "We forgot our picnic lunch," Mom _____.

4. "We must have left it at the _____ of the driveway."

sale   sail

5. We bought a boat at the _____.

6. Now we can _____ out to sea.

right   write

7. I'll _____ a special letter to my friend in Texas.

8. I'll mail it _____ after lunch.

road   rode   rowed

9. We _____ to the country in our car.

10. It began to rain, and the _____ became flooded.

11. Maybe we should have _____ home!

Gail says...

Last Saturday I was helping my mother with a yard sale. I made a sign that said, "Don't miss the greatest sail of your life!"

In no time a family stopped by. They said they couldn't wait to ride in our boat. That's when I figured out that I should have written **sale** instead of **sail**. They were so disappointed.

Spelling Matters!

Spelling Words

car	party
far	hard
arm	heart *LOOKOUT WORD*
farm	dark
star	mark
start	park
smart	yard
part	

Review	Challenge
aunt	startled
man	carpenter
hand	

My Words

_____

_____

_____

_____

Learn and Spell

Words With ar

A See and Say

The Spelling Concept

/är/   p**ar**ty   c**ar**

When a word has /är/, the sound is spelled **ar**.

It's very odd to find an *ear* in h*ear*t!

MEMORY JOGGER

B Link Sounds and Letters

Say each spelling word. Listen for /är/. Look at each word. Where do you see **ar**? Sort the spelling words on a chart like this one.

Word Sort

ar__	__ar__	__ar	Other Words

C Write and Check

Which words in the riddle have /är/? Write the one that is a spelling word.

_____

RIDDLE

What would this country be if everyone drove a pink car?

(a pink carnation! (car nation))

Vocabulary Practice

Ⓐ Build Vocabulary: **Related Words**

Write the spelling word that belongs in each group.

1. ranch, dairy, ___
2. leg, neck, ___
3. clever, wise, ___
4. truck, bus, ___
5. celebration, festival, ___
6. sun, moon, ___
7. playground, garden, ___

Spell Chat

Think of another group that has an ar word. Challenge the person behind you to guess the ar word.

Ⓑ Word Study: **Compound Words**

A compound word is made up of two words put together, for example, **rain** + **bow** = **rainbow**. Match a word in A with a word in B to make a compound word. Write the new word.

A	B
8. far	yard
9. heart	away
10. back	ship
11. dark	room
12. book	beat
13. hard	mark

Ⓒ Write

Use these spelling words to write the first two lines of a song or poem.

start   part   hand

_____

_____

Be a Spelling Sleuth

Look in science articles and magazines for words with ar, such as **star**, **garden**, and **dark**. Make a list of them.

Spelling Words

car	party
far	hard
arm	heart
farm	dark
star	mark
start	park
smart	yard
part	

Review	Challenge
aunt	startled
man	carpenter
hand	

My Words

_____

_____

_____

_____

Spelling Words

car	party
far	hard
arm	heart LOOKOUT WORD
farm	dark
star	mark
start	park
smart	yard
part	

Review	Challenge
aunt	startled
man	carpenter
hand	

My Words

_____

_____

_____

Quick Write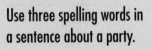
Use three spelling words in a sentence about a party.

Write and Proofread

You may wish to do this activity on a computer.

A Write Captions

Sometimes you can tell a story through pictures and captions. First, draw or imagine three pictures of a family party or picnic. Then, write one sentence for each picture. Use three spelling words.

Tip
Capitalize the names of people.

B Proofread

Joe wrote these captions for some family photos. He made two spelling errors. One of them is an incorrect homophone. He also made one punctuation error and forgot to capitalize a person's name. Correct the errors.

What a great party we had in our backyard

We had a cake in the shape of a hart.

Here we are at the start of a race. Ant rita said, "1, 2, 3, Go!"

We played until it was nearly dark.

PROOFREADING MARKS

∧ Add
⊙ Add a period
ℓ Take out
⌒∧ Move
≡ Capital letter
/ Small letter
¶ Indent paragraph

Now proofread your captions.
Check for spelling, punctuation, and capitalization.

Ⓐ Use a Dictionary: **Example Sentence**

The dictionary lists the meanings of a word. Sometimes it also gives a sentence that shows how the word can be used. Here is a dictionary entry for **far**.

> **far** /fär/ *adverb* A great distance. *Have you traveled far?*

Write another example sentence for **far**.

_____

_____

Read the dictionary entry for **start**.

> **start** /stärt/ *verb* To begin to do something.

Now write your own example sentence for **start**.

_____

_____

Ⓑ Test Yourself

What letters are missing? Write the whole spelling word.

1. _ _ m	6. st _ _ t	11. h _ _ _ t
2. c _ _	7. sm _ _ t	12. m _ _ k
3. f _ _	8. p _ _ k	13. p _ _ ty
4. f _ _ m	9. p _ _ t	14. h _ _ d
5. st _ _	10. y _ _ d	15. d _ _ k

For Tomorrow...
Get ready to share the ar words you discovered, and remember to study for your test!

Get Word Wise

The word **car** comes from a Latin word **carrus**, meaning "chariot." A chariot was a small, fast cart pulled by horses. In the late 1800s, Americans began using the word for a new invention—the automobile.

Word Study Strategy

See the word

Say it slowly

Link sounds and letters

Write

Check

Words With ear

Ⓐ See and Say

Spelling Words

bear	clear
pear	hear
wear	heard
tear LOOKOUT WORD	learn
ear	earth
dear	earn
fear	early
near	

Review	Challenge
heart	appear
weak	earthquake
where	

My Words

_____

_____

_____

_____

The Spelling Concept

/âr/	bear
/ēr/	hear
/ûr/	heard

The letters **ear** can stand for three different vowel sounds, /âr/, /ēr/, or /ûr/.

> Boo-hoo! A tear!
> R-r-r-i-p! A tear!
> Same spelling,
> different sound.

MEMORY JOGGER

Ⓑ Link Sounds and Letters

Say each spelling word. Listen to the sound made by the letters **ear**. Then sort the words on the chart by the way they sound.

Word Sort

a tear in her shirt	a tear in your eye	earn money

Ⓒ Write and Check

Which word in the brain teaser has **ear** in it? Write another spelling word that rhymes with it.

_____

_____

BRAIN TEASER

What is big and white and found in Texas?

a lost polar bear

Vocabulary Practice

A Build Vocabulary: Synonyms

Synonyms are words that have the same or almost the same meaning. For example, **jump** and **leap** are synonyms. Write the spelling word that is a synonym for each of these words.

1. close
2. rip
3. study
4. loved
5. soil
6. soon

> **Spell Chat**
> Challenge the person next to you to think of three synonyms for **earth**.

B Word Study: Verbs

Read each sentence. Write the spelling word that is the present-tense form for each past-tense verb.

7. I <u>earned</u> a dollar for helping my dad wash the car.

8. I <u>learned</u> to skate at the roller rink.

9. I <u>cleared</u> my desk to do my homework.

10. I <u>feared</u> that it might rain very hard.

11. I <u>heard</u> Juan singing his favorite songs.

12. I <u>wore</u> a jacket to the school play.

C Write

Write a funny sentence, using these spelling words.

heard   bear   pear   ear

_____

_____

_____

Be a Spelling Sleuth

Look at posters and signs around your neighborhood for words with the letters *ear*, such as **near, wear,** and **hear.**

Spelling Words

bear	clear
pear	hear
wear	heard
tear *(Lookout Word)*	learn
ear	earth
dear	earn
fear	early
near	

Review	Challenge
heart	appear
weak	earthquake
where	

My Words

_____

_____

_____

_____

Spelling Words

bear	clear
pear	hear
wear	heard
tear	learn
ear	earth
dear	earn
fear	early
near	

tear — LOOKOUT WORD

Review	Challenge
heart	appear
weak	earthquake
where	

My Words

_____

_____

_____

_____

Quick Write

Use at least three spelling words to describe what you might see, hear, and smell in a forest.

You may wish to do this activity on a computer.

A Write a Description

Write a description of a person or an animal in a folktale. What does the character look like? How does the character act? Use your imagination and at least three spelling words.

Tip
Read your sentences aloud to make sure the words are in the right order.

B Proofread

Alison wrote a folktale. She made three spelling errors. In one sentence, she also made a mistake in the word order. Correct Alison's mistakes.

> Alex was a big brown bear who liked to ware a red hat. He lived near the river. Every morning he would get up erly and pears eat. He had a kind hart, but everyone feared him because his growl was so loud. You could hear it halfway round the earth.

PROOFREADING MARKS

∧ Add
⊙ Add a period
ℓ Take out
○∧ Move
≡ Capital letter
/ Small letter
¶ Indent paragraph

Now proofread your description. Check for spelling and word order.

A Use the Dictionary: **Word Meaning**

To find out what a word means, you look it up in the dictionary. Here is a dictionary entry for **pear.**

pear /pâr/ *noun*
A juicy, sweet, yellow, green, red, or brown fruit with a smooth skin.

Read the dictionary entries below. Write the spelling word that matches each meaning.

_____ *adjective* Easy to be seen through.

_____ *noun* The part of the body used for hearing.

_____ *verb* To receive payment for work done.

_____ *verb* To sense sounds through your ears.

B Test Yourself

Use the code to figure out each spelling word. Then write the word.

a	b	c	d	e	f	h	l	n	p	r	t	w	y
1	2	3	4	5	6	8	12	14	16	18	20	23	25

1. 5-1-18
2. 14-5-1-18
3. 20-5-1-18
4. 5-1-18-20-8
5. 6-5-1-18

6. 5-1-18-14
7. 5-1-18-12-25
8. 4-5-1-18
9. 3-12-5-1-18
10. 2-5-1-18

11. 16-5-1-18
12. 23-5-1-18
13. 8-5-1-18
14. 12-5-1-18-14
15. 8-5-1-18-4

For Tomorrow...
Get ready to share all the ear *words you discovered, and remember to study for your test!*

Get Word Wise

The word **earn** comes from the Old German word for **harvest,** **arnōn**. Long ago, people didn't earn money. Everything they needed came from the crops they grew and harvested.

Word Study Strategy

START

See the word

Say it slowly

Link sounds and letters

Write

Check

END

Words With c or k

Ⓐ See and Say

Spelling Words

camp	key LOOKOUT WORD
camera	kids
cave	kindergarten
color	kiss
cost	kitchen
contest	kite
cub	kitten
keep	

Review	Challenge
tear	ketchup
kind	catsup
coat	

My Words

_____

_____

_____

_____

The Spelling Concept

c	camp	color	cub
k	keep	kitten	

Both the letters **c** and **k** can stand for /k/. The /k/ sound is spelled with a **c** before **a**, **o**, and **u**. It is spelled with a **k** before **e** and **i**.

> A kitten with a k becomes a cat with a c.
>
> MEMORY JOGGER

Ⓑ Link Sounds and Letters

Say each spelling word. Listen for /k/. Look at each word to see whether /k/ is spelled with a **c** or a **k**. Sort the words on a chart like this one.

Word Sort

cat 🐱	kitten 🐈

Ⓒ Write and Check

Write the spelling words in the tongue twister that have /k/. Then, write your own tongue twister, using spelling words.

TONGUE TWISTER
Can the kids keep a kitten, cub, and kangaroo in the kitchen? Of course not!

_____ _____

_____ _____

_____

A Build Vocabulary: **Rhyming Words**

It's time to rhyme. Write a spelling word that rhymes with each word below.

1. mitten
2. sea
3. rub
4. lids
5. bite
6. gave

Spell Chat
Challenge a partner to think of rhymes for three other spelling words.

B Word Study: **Action Verbs**

An action word tells what the subject of a sentence does. Find the action verb in each sentence. Write the verb.

7. We camp in the woods for a week every year.
8. It doesn't cost very much.
9. I always kiss my dog good-bye.
10. We keep our flashlight close by in our tent.
11. Sometimes I color pictures of the woods.

C Write

Write a poster that a third-grade class might make for a **kindergarten** art **contest**. The prizes are a **camera** and a play **kitchen**. Use the highlighted words.

_____

_____

_____

Be a Spelling Sleuth

In the supermarket or at home, look at food labels for words that begin with the letters c or k, such as **kitchen, carrots,** and **kiwi.** Keep a list.

Spelling Words

camp	key LOOKOUT WORD
camera	kids
cave	kindergarten
color	kiss
cost	kitchen
contest	kite
cub	kitten
keep	

Review	Challenge
tear	ketchup
kind	catsup
coat	

My Words

_____

_____

_____

_____

Spelling Words

camp	key
camera	kids
cave	kindergarten
color	kiss
cost	kitchen
contest	kite
cub	kitten
keep	

Review	Challenge
tear	ketchup
kind	catsup
coat	

My Words

Quick Write
Use two spelling words to write two sentences about a favorite book.

You may wish to do this activity on a computer.

A Write an Article
What would you like to read? Write an article about a school book fair. Include some book titles in your paragraph. Use at least three spelling words.

Tip
The titles of books should be underlined. If you're using a computer, use italics.

B Proofread
Diego wrote an article about a book fair. He made two spelling errors, one capitalization error, and one error in underlining. Correct the errors.

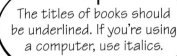

> last Monday Mari went to the book fair. Everyone was there. She even saw kids from kindergarten. There were so many books. Mari bought three. First, she found <u>The Lion Cub in the Kichen.</u> Then, she picked up <u>How to Use a Camra</u> and The Red Coat. What luck! Mari had found three great books.

PROOFREADING MARKS
∧ Add
⊙ Add a period
ꬁ Take out
ᓬ Move
≡ Capital letter
/ Small letter
¶ Indent paragraph

Now proofread your article. Check for spelling, capitalization, and underlining of titles.

A Use the Dictionary: **Two Definitions**

One word can have more than one definition. The dictionary gives each meaning a number. Read the dictionary entries for **keep** and **key**.

> **keep** /kēp/ *verb*
> **1.** To have something and not get rid of it. **2.** To stay the same.

> **key** /kē/ *noun*
> **1.** A piece of metal shaped to fit into a lock to open it or to start an engine. **2.** One of the buttons on a computer or typewriter.

Decide which meaning of the word fits the sentence. Write the number of the meaning of **keep** or **key** in each sentence.

_____ We ran around to keep warm.

_____ Ann hit the wrong key and typed **j** instead of **k**.

_____ Let's keep these books.

_____ Carl turned the key to lock the door.

B Test Yourself

Figure out which letters are missing. Write each spelling word.

1. c _ _ e
2. c _ _ t
3. k _ ss
4. k _ tch _ n
5. c _ _ t _ _ t

6. k _ _ p
7. k _ y
8. c _ _ p
9. c _ m _ _ a
10. k _ ds

11. c _ l _ r
12. k _ _ dergar _ _ n
13. k _ tt _ n
14. k _ _ e
15. c _ b

> **For Tomorrow...**
> Get ready to share the c and k words you discovered, and remember to study for your test!

Get Word Wise

Some people write **ketchup** and others write **catsup.** Both these words come from the name of a fish sauce, **ke-tsiap,** used in China. Sometime later, someone thought it was a good idea to add tomatoes to the sauce.

Word Study Strategy

See the word

Say it slowly

Link sounds and letters

Write

Check

START

END

Spelling Words

safe	sunset
season	cell
sell	cent
sent	center
seven	celebrate
silly	city
sister	recess 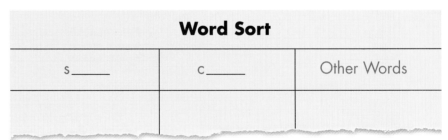 LOOKOUT WORD
soft	

Review	Challenge
key	science
beside	scissors
save	

My Words

_____

_____

_____

_____

_____

Learn and Spell

Words With s or c

A See and Say

The Spelling Concept

s	safe	silly
c	cent	city

There are two ways to spell /s/. It can be spelled with **s** before any letter. It can also be spelled with **c**, but only before **e** or **i**.

> Last season, I swam in the sea.

MEMORY JOGGER

B Link Sounds and Letters

Say each spelling word. Listen for /s/. Look at each word to see whether /s/ is spelled with **s** or **c**. Sort the words on a chart like this one.

Word Sort

s_____	c_____	Other Words

C Write and Check

Write the spelling words in the tongue twister.

_____

_____

TONGUE TWISTER

Sam and Sue sell shells by the seashore at sunset.

A Build Vocabulary: **Classify**

What do the words in each group below have in common? Figure it out. Then write the spelling word that belongs with the group.

1. sent, scent, ___
2. three, five, ___
3. brother, mother, ___
4. midnight, sunrise, ___
5. goofy, funny, ___
6. village, town, ___

7. winter, summer, ___
8. gentle, smooth, ___
9. celebrating, celebrated, ___
10. room, locked, ___
11. rest, break, ___

B Word Study: **Prefixes**

Read each sentence. Write the spelling word that could be added to the prefix in the sentence.

Spell Chat
Challenge the person behind you to think of two other words with /s/ that include the prefix re- or un-.

center   safe   sell   sent

12. The used car dealer will <u>re</u> ___ your old car.

13. I <u>re</u> ___ the letter since you didn't get it.

14. It is <u>un</u> ___ to ride a bike without a helmet.

15. Juan used a computer to <u>re</u> ___ the word on the page.

C Write

Write a sentence about what you would like to do at recess. Use a Spelling Word, Review Word, or one of your My Words.

___

___

Be a Spelling Sleuth

Look at street and traffic signs around town for words that begin with c or s and have /s/, such as **slow** and **city**.

Spelling Words

safe	sunset
season	cell
sell	cent
sent	center
seven	celebrate
silly	city
sister	recess
soft	

Review	Challenge
key	science
beside	scissors
save	

My Words

___

___

___

___

Spelling Words

safe	sunset
season	cell
sell	cent
sent	center
seven	celebrate
silly	city
sister	recess LOOKOUT WORD
soft	

Review	Challenge
key	science
beside	scissors
save	

My Words

_____

_____

_____

_____

Quick Write

Write a sentence that is something you might say to a friend. See if you can use as many as five words with /s/.

You may wish to do this activity on a computer.

A Write Dialogue

Make your favorite story character speak! Choose a character and write a conversation you two might have. Be sure to use quotation marks to show the character's exact words. Include three spelling words.

B Proofread

Sarah wrote this dialogue with her favorite character, Ms. Frizzle. She made three spelling errors and two punctuation errors. Correct them.

Tip
Quotation marks go before the speaker's first word and after the punctuation mark.

> "Ms. Frizzle!" I cried. "It's you! Your books really make me love science.
>
> "Science is fun," said Ms. Frizzle. "That's the kee."
>
> I just read about your trip to the senter of the earth. You always take us to the hottest places," I said.
>
> She smiled. "We always come back saf and sound. That's the best part!"

PROOFREADING MARKS

∧ Add
⊙ Add a period
ℓ Take out
ↄↄ Move
≡ Capital letter
∕ Small letter
¢ Indent paragraph

Now proofread your dialogue. Check your spelling and punctuation. Be sure you used quotation marks correctly.

Ⓐ Use a Dictionary: Homophones

Homophones are words that sound alike but are spelled differently. They have different meanings, too. To choose the word you want, you must know its meaning. Read the dictionary entries for these homophones.

> **cent** /sent/ *noun*
> A unit of money. One hundred cents equal one dollar.

> **sent** /sent/ *verb*
> Past tense of **send**. Made something go somewhere.

Write the homophone that completes each sentence.

Gila _____ a letter to her grandfather.

I saw a shiny new _____ on the sidewalk.

Ⓑ Test Yourself

Write the spelling word for each clue.

1. a penny
2. large town
3. a locked strong box
4. to party
5. winter or spring
6. opposite of buy
7. a number
8. goofy
9. a brother or a _____
10. a break
11. not hard
12. mailed a letter
13. evening
14. in the middle
15. rhymes with bell and starts with c

For Tomorrow...
Get ready to share the words with s and c you discovered, and remember to study for your test!

Get Word Wise
The word **cent** comes from the Latin word **centum**, which means 100. There are 100 cents in a dollar. How many years are in a century?

Word Study Strategy

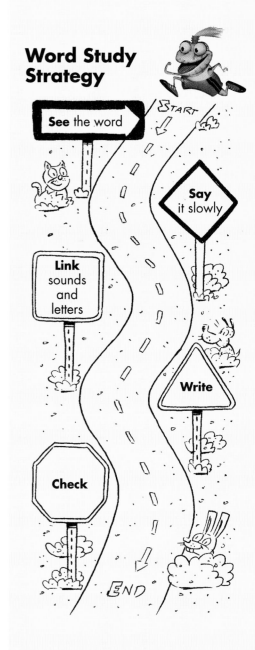

See the word
Say it slowly
Link sounds and letters
Write
Check

Words With ck or k

A See and Say

Spelling Words

back	creek
pack	leak
neck	speak
trick	break
cricket	oak
lock	croak
block	shook
clock	

LOOKOUT WORD

Review	Challenge
recess	freckles
soak	chuckle
drink	

My Words

_____

_____

_____

_____

The Spelling Concept

ck	back	cricket
k	shook	croak

When /k/ follows a short vowel sound, it is usually spelled **ck** as in **back**. When /k/ follows a vowel sound that is spelled with two letters, it is spelled **k** as in **shook** and **croak**.

ea = long *e*
But **break** breaks the rule.

MEMORY JOGGER

B Link Sounds and Letters

Say each spelling word. Look at each word to see whether /k/ is spelled with **ck** or **k**. Then sort the words on a chart like this.

Word Sort

short vowel + ck	two-letter vowel sounds + k

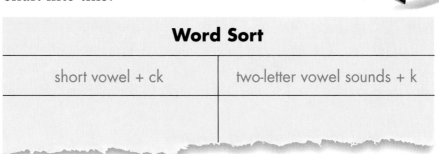

C Write and Check

Write the two spelling words in the rhyme.

_____

_____

NO JOKE!

In Flapjack Swamp,
And it's no joke,
A frog can chirp,
And a cricket can croak!

A Build Vocabulary: **Action Verbs**

An action verb tells what someone or something does. Write the spelling word that tells the action in each sentence.

croak   leak   pack   shook   speak   trick

1. Anna will _____ her clothes for the trip.

2. Hank will _____ to the class about his new pet.

3. Can you hear the frogs _____ late at night?

4. My dog can _____ my cat.

5. Fix the hole in the roof, or the roof will _____.

6. The earthquake _____ the house.

B Word Study: **Compound Words**

Find the two words in each compound word. Write the word that is a spelling word.

7. necktie

8. locksmith

9. clockwise

10. blockbuster

11. outbreak

12–13. backpack

C Write

Use these words in a sentence about a walk in the woods.

cricket   creek   oak

_____

_____

Spell Chat
Ask the person next to you to think of three other verbs that end with /k/.

Be a Spelling Sleuth
Look in bookstores or on your bookshelves at home for book titles with k or ck.

Spelling Words

back	creek
pack	leak
neck	speak
trick	break LOOKOUT WORD
cricket	oak
lock	croak
block	shook
clock	

Review	Challenge
recess	freckles
soak	chuckle
drink	

My Words

_____

_____

_____

_____

Spelling Words

back	creek
pack	leak
neck	speak
trick	break *LOOKOUT WORD*
cricket	oak
lock	croak
block	shook
clock	

Review	Challenge
recess	freckles
soak	chuckle
drink	

My Words

_____

_____

_____

Quick Write

Use two spelling words in a sentence about a clever trick a pet might do.

You may wish to do this activity on a computer.

Ⓐ Write a Character Sketch

Make up an animal character. Write a paragraph that tells about the character. What does it look like? What does it like to do? Use as many spelling words as you can.

Ⓑ Proofread

Nina wrote a paragraph about a character she made up. She made three spelling errors and two errors in capitalization.

Tip
Remember to begin each word that names a specific person, place, or thing with a capital letter.

Jack Dogwings is a small black and white mutt. jack has a long nek and big floppy ears. On his bak is a pair of wings. He likes to fly high above the trees. He also loves to soack in the creek. Jack's best friend is a flying cat named sam.

PROOFREADING MARKS

∧ Add
⊙ Add a period
ℓ Take out
⌒ Move
≡ Capital letter
／ Small letter
¢ Indent paragraph

Now proofread your character sketch. Check for spelling and capitalization.

A Use the Dictionary: **Word Endings**

To find words with the endings -**ing** and -**ed** added, look under the base word. Read the dictionary entry for **pack**.

> **pack** /pak/ *verb*
> To put objects into a box, case, or bag. **packing, packed**

Write the word **pack** with the endings -**ing** and -**ed**.

_____   _____

Write the entry word you would look up to find each word with an ending.

leaking _____   locking _____

croaked _____   tricked _____

speaking _____   blocked _____

B Test Yourself

Think of how to spell /k/ in each of these words. Write each word.

1. tri___
2. lo___
3. shoo___
4. ne___
5. spea___
6. ba___
7. lea___
8. blo___
9. pa___
10. brea___

11. cree___
12. cri___et
13. oa___
14. clo___
15. croa___

For Tomorrow...
Get ready to share words with ck or k that you've discovered, and remember to study for your test!

Get Word Wise

Think about the sounds frogs and crickets make. A frog makes a sound that's a lot like the word **croak**. A cricket makes sounds like the name **cricket**. Both words are called imitative words. That means they sound like the things they name.

Word Study Strategy

START

See the word

Say it slowly

Link sounds and letters

Write

Check

END

Go Fly a Kite !

Complete each sentence with a word from the box.

kite   city   color   celebrate   park

Did you know that (1) flying is popular all over the world? It's one way people (2) spring. Look up on a breezy spring day, and you may see kites of every (3) . The beach is a good place for kite flying. In a (4) like Los Angeles, people go to the (5) to fly their kites.

clear   earth   near   season   sent

The first kites were not toys. In China, people (6) messages far and (7) with kites. In Korea even today, children write sayings such as "Come good luck" on their kites. In Thailand, people fly kites at the end of the rainy (8) to make the clouds go away. Their kites seem to soar high above the (9) . The people like to see (10) skies after so much rain.

star   contest   keep   trick   break

In Japan and in Thailand, kite flyers may win prizes in a kite flying (11) . The (12) is to (13) their kites safe while flying them against other kites. People in Thailand fly large (14) -shaped kites, called **chulas**. They use their kites to pull the other kites down. In Japan, children try to (15) the strings of other kites. No matter who wins, everyone has fun.

arm
yard
seven
creek
kids
star
kitchen
lock

What Is It?

Write the spelling word that goes with each clue.

1. A key will open it. _____

2. My dog likes to bury bones in it. _____

3. It's near the dining room. _____

4. It's larger than a brook and smaller than a river. _____

5. An octopus has more than one. _____

6. It's another name for young goats. _____

7. It's between six and eight. _____

8. It has five points and shines. _____

Synonyms

silly   clock   wear
speak   city   shook

Write the spelling word that means the same thing or almost the same thing as the words below.

9. foolish, funny, _____

10. moved, trembled, _____

11. put on, dress in, _____

12. talk, say, _____

13. town, village, _____

14. watch, timepiece, _____

Word Ladder

Go from **cave** to **park**. Change just one letter at a time to make a new word. The box shows which letter has been changed.

cave

_ _ ☐ _

☐ _ _ _

_ _ _ ☐

park

far
star
smart
party
learn
kitten
park
dark

clock
contest
seven
sunset
bear
cricket
cave

Tip
Begin the first and last words, and each important word in a title with a capital letter.

The Name Game

A catchy title grabs our interest. What do you think a movie called **The Kitten Contest** might be about? Think of some more titles. Use two or more spelling words in each title.

1. A funny movie

_____

2. An animal cartoon

_____

3. A song

_____

4. A computer game

_____

5. A mystery story

_____

Look back at My Words and the words you misspelled in your Unit 2 Posttests. Use them to write more titles.

6. A folk tale

_____

Ad Time

Write a short ad for one of your titles. Proofread it for spelling, capitalization, and punctuation. Then make it into a poster.

_____

_____

Can You "C" It?

Sometimes the letter **c** has /s/. Other times it has /k/. Write the spelling word that fits each set of clues.

> celebrate   center   recess   camp
> cub   color   cave   cent

1. It begins with **c** and ends with **r**. It means the middle of something. _____

2. This word begins with **c** and ends with **e**. This is where a bear may spend the winter. _____

3. Here's a word that begins with **c** and ends with **r**. Purple is an example of this word. _____

4. It begins with **c** and ends with **t**. It's another name for a penny. _____

5. It's a word that begins with **c** and has just one syllable. It is a young lion, wolf, or bear. _____

6. This word begins with **r** and ends with **s**. It is the part of the school day when you aren't studying.

   _____

7. Here's a word that begins with **c** and has three syllables. You may do this on a special occasion. _____

8. It begins with **c** and ends with **p**. You may find a tent and sleeping bags here. _____

Josh says...

Yesterday my friend had a sidewalk sale. She wrote a sign. It said, **One Sent Sale. Buy two pencils for a penny**. I told her, "You used the wrong **sent**. The word for penny is spelled c-e-n-t."

My friend thanked me and changed the sign. Now it reads **One Cent Sale.** Then she even gave me a free pencil. It didn't cost me a cent. It pays to spell well.

Spelling Matters!

Learn and Spell

Words With j or g

A See and Say

Spelling Words

jacket	jump
jar	just
jeans	gentle
jelly	general
jet	giant
job	giraffe
joke	gym *LOOKOUT WORD*
judge	

Review	Challenge
break	jungle
yawn	gigantic
eight	

My Words

_____

_____

_____

The Spelling Concept

j   jar   jump

g   gentle   giant   gym

The sound /j/ can be spelled with the letter **j** or **g**. **J** can be used before any letter. **G** is only used when the next letter is **e**, **i**, or **y**.

> What are the world's largest insects? Giants!
>
> MEMORY JOGGER

B Link Sounds and Letters

Say each spelling word and listen for /j/. Is /j/ spelled with a **j** or a **g**? Look at each word to see how it is spelled. Sort the spelling words on a chart like the one below.

Word Sort

j___	ge___	gi___	gy___

C Write and Check

Read the riddle. Write the words that have /j/.

_____

_____

RIDDLE

Why did the judge call the race a tie?

The giraffe twins finished neck and neck.

FINISH

A Build Vocabulary: **Compound Words**

Compound words are two words put together. They have a meaning all their own. A hot dog is a frank, not a dog that is hot!

Write the spelling word that is one part of each compound word.

1. a wasp = a yellow _____

2. bright-colored candy = _____ beans

3. denim pants = blue _____

4. a flying machine = a _____ plane

5. metal bars to swing or climb on = a jungle _____

6. a book of funny stories = a _____ book

7. a cord used to play a game = a _____ rope

B Word Study: **Word Patterns**

Write the spelling words that answer each clue.

8. rhymes with car

9. begins like jump and ends like Bob

10. rhymes with fudge

11. has us in the middle

12. has a g and three consonants together

13. has ant in it

14. has a g and a double letter

15. every other letter is a vowel

C Write

Write a funny sentence using these words.

giant   jar

_____

_____

Spell Chat

Ask the person next to you to think of another compound word. At least one of the words should begin with /j/.

Be a Spelling Sleuth

Look for names that begin with /j/ on street signs, such as "Gingerbread Road," and store signs such as "Jack and Jill's Pharmacy."

Spelling Words

jacket	jump
jar	just
jeans	gentle
jelly	general
jet	giant
job	giraffe
joke	gym
judge	

Review	Challenge
break	jungle
yawn	gigantic
eight	

My Words

_____

_____

_____

_____

Spelling Words

jacket	jump
jar	just
jeans	gentle
jelly	general
jet	giant
job	giraffe
joke	gym LOOKOUT WORD
judge	

Review	Challenge
break	jungle
yawn	gigantic
eight	

My Words

Quick Write

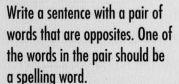

Write a sentence with a pair of words that are opposites. One of the words in the pair should be a spelling word.

A Write a Fantasy

 You may wish to do this activity on a computer.

Imagine a land in which everyone does things backward. Write about what might happen. Use three spelling words in your fantasy. Be sure the words are in the right order so that your sentences make sense.

> **Tip**
> To tell what happened in the past, most verbs need **-ed**.

B Proofread

Ryan wrote about a fair in Backward Land. He made two spelling errors and one punctuation error. In one sentence, the words are not in the right order. Correct the errors.

> First, the general told jokes that made everyone cry Then, the ant huge raced with the tiny giant. Nearby, a worm jumpd over eigt crawling frogs. The judge gave a trophy to the loser. Everyone whispered, "Yeah!"

PROOFREADING MARKS

∧ Add
⊙ Add a period
ℓ Take out
◯↗ Move
≡ Capital letter
／ Small letter
¶ Indent paragraph

Now proofread your sentences. Check for spelling, punctuation, and correct word order.

A Use the Dictionary: **Syllables**

Look at this dictionary entry for **general**. The word **general** has three vowel sounds so it has three syllables. In the dictionary, you will see the entry word divided into three parts, or syllables.

> **gen•er•al** /jen ər əl/
> **1.** *adjective* To do with everyone or everything. **2.** *adjective* Not specific. **3.** *noun* A high-ranking military officer.

Say these spelling words. How many vowel sounds do you hear? Write the number of syllables in each word in the ( ). Check the Spelling Dictionary to see if you have the correct number. Then write the word in syllables.

jelly _____ ( ) _____   gentle _____ ( ) _____

jeans _____ ( ) _____   giant _____ ( ) _____

jacket _____ ( ) _____   giraffe _____ ( ) _____

B Test Yourself

Write a spelling word for each clue.

1. pants
2. work
3. plane
4. person who decides
5. to hop
6. funny story
7. jam
8. army leader
9. short coat
10. bottle
11. very big
12. place to work out
13. mild
14. only
15. animal

For Tomorrow...
Get ready to share the words with j or g that you discovered. Remember to study for the test!

Word Study Strategy

START

See the word

Say it slowly

Link sounds and letters

Write

Check

END

Spelling Words

gas	giggle
game	gum
gate	guard
gave	guess
garden	guest
garbage	guide
garage LOOKOUT WORD	guy
geese	

Review	Challenge
gym	guardian
yard	language
grow	

My Words

_____

_____

_____

_____

Words With g or gu

A See and Say

The Spelling Concept

g	gate	garden
gu	guest	guide

The sound /g/ is usually spelled with the letter **g**.
Sometimes /g/ is made with the letters **gu**.

G, u make a great guard! (Gee, you make a great guard!)

MEMORY JOGGER

B Link Sounds and Letters

Look at each spelling word, and say it aloud. How is /g/ spelled in each word? Is it **g** as in **game** or **gu** as in **guard**? Sort the spelling words.

Word Sort

g——	gu——

C Write and Check

Find the words in the tongue twister that have /g/. Then use three spelling words to write your own tongue twister.

TONGUE TWISTER
The gabby guest gazed at geese in the garden.
Say it as fast as you can!

_____

_____

_____

A Build Vocabulary: **Words Inside Words**

Find the Spelling Word or Review Word hidden in each of these words. Take away one letter. For example, take away the **a** in **ago** to make **go.** Write each word.

1. glum   4. grave
2. gasp   5. grown
3. grate   6. garbage

B Word Study: **Plurals**

You can make most words plural by adding **-s,** as in **girls.** Some plurals are irregular. For example, **geese** is the plural of **goose.** Read the sentences. Write the plural of each word in ( ).

7. Four (guy) discovered an old hotel.

8. When did the last (guest) stay there?

9. The (garden) were covered with weeds.

10. Only the (goose) wandered across the yard.

11. The (gate) were locked, and the hotel looked empty.

12. There were (garage) in the back of the hotel.

13. Let's play some (game) on the lawn.

14. "You can't stay!" said the (guard).

15. Only (guide) can bring visitors here.

C Write

Write two funny questions using the words **garbage, giggle,** and **guess.**

_____

_____

_____

Be a Spelling Sleuth
Keep your eyes open for words that begin with g or gu, such as **goldfish** or **guitar,** in magazines and books. Keep a list.

Spell Chat
Turn to a classmate. How many spelling words can he or she make with the letters in _Galveston's Greatest Guide?_

Spelling Words

gas	giggle
game	gum
gate	guard
gave	guess
garden	guest
garbage	guide
garage LOOKOUT WORD	guy
geese	

Review	Challenge
gym	guardian
yard	language
grow	

My Words

_____

_____

_____

_____

You may wish to do this activity on a computer.

Spelling Words

gas	giggle
game	gum
gate	guard
gave	guess
garden	guest
garbage	guide
garage LOOKOUT WORD	guy
geese	

Review	Challenge
gym	guardian
yard	language
grow	

My Words

_____

_____

_____

Quick Write

Make up a title for a how-to book. Use one or more spelling words.

A Write a How-To Paragraph

Teach a friend how to do something. Write a how-to paragraph. First, think of something you can do well. Next, list the steps in order. Then, write your how-to paragraph. Use three spelling words. Remember to indent the first line.

B Proofread

Keisha wrote a good how-to paragraph. However, she misspelled three words and didn't indent her paragraph. Keisha also forgot to make a word plural. Correct her errors.

Tip
When you form plurals, remember this. Most plural words end in **s**.

> Here is how to plant a vegetable guarden in your yad. Carrots are easy to grow. First, dig several small holes. Next, put a seed in each hole. Then, cover the seeds with soil. Water the seeds every day. Gess what? Soon you'll have carrot to eat.

PROOFREADING MARKS

∧ Add
⊙ Add a period
ℓ Take out
↻↗ Move
≡ Capital letter
/ Small letter
¶ Indent paragraph

Now proofread your paragraph. Check for spelling, punctuation, and plurals. Make sure you indented the first line.

Get Word Wise

What's the difference between a garden and a yard? They mean different things to us now, but both words come from a Latin word **garda** that meant "enclosed place."

Ⓐ Use the Dictionary: **Stressed Syllables**

A dictionary pronunciation shows you how to say a word. It uses special letters and symbols. When a word has more than one syllable, the syllable in dark type gets more stress.

> **ga•rage** /gə **räzh** *or* gə **räj**/ *noun*
> A building where cars are kept.

> **gar•bage** /**gär** bij/ *noun*
> Food and other things that are thrown out.

Study each pronunciation. If the second syllable is the stressed syllable, write the word after **garage.** If the first syllable is stressed, write the word after **garbage.**

ga•zelle /gə **zel**/   **gar•den** /**gär** dən/
gig•gle /**gig** əl/   **gi•raffe** /jə **raf**/

garage _____   _____

garbage _____   _____

Ⓑ Test Yourself

Read each clue. Then write the spelling word.

1. you chew it
2. trash
3. part of a fence
4. visitor
5. used in cars
6. flower beds
7. past of give
8. you play it
9. watch over
10. plural of **goose**
11. show the way
12. think
13. silly laugh
14. place for cars
15. boy or man

Word Study Strategy

START
See the word
Say it slowly
Link sounds and letters
Write
Check
END

For Tomorrow...
Get ready to share the /g/ words you discovered, and remember to study for your test!

Spelling Words

age	ridge
cage	bridge
page	edge
stage	ledge
large	bandage
change	village
budge	college *LOOKOUT WORD*
fudge	

Review	Challenge
garage	challenge
huge	manage
earn	

My Words

_____

_____

_____

_____

Words With ge or dge

A See and Say

The Spelling Concept

dge	fudge	edge
ge	page	large

Many words end with /j/. After short vowels, this sound is usually spelled **dge**. After long vowels and after consonants, this sound is usually spelled **ge**.

> The **d** in fu**d**ge makes it really **d**elicious.

MEMORY JOGGER

B Link Sounds and Letters

Say each spelling word. Listen for the final /j/. Is /j/ spelled **ge** or **dge**? Sort the spelling words on a web like this one.

Word Sort

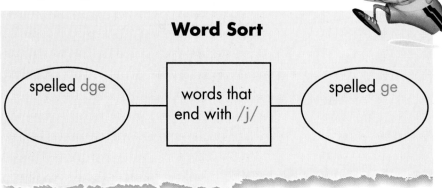

spelled dge — words that end with /j/ — spelled ge

C Write and Check

Which words in the joke end with /j/? Write the two that are spelling words.

_____

_____

JOKE

Why did the doctor keep her large bandage in the refrigerator?

She wanted to use it for cold cuts.

A Build Vocabulary: **Synonyms**

A synonym is a word that has almost the same meaning as another word. Read each sentence. Write the spelling word that is a synonym for each underlined word.

1. Last week we went to the <u>town</u> fair.

2. The fair was so crowded, I could hardly <u>move</u>.

3. It wasn't as busy along the <u>side</u> of the street.

4. My ride on the <u>big</u> Ferris wheel was great!

5. We loved hearing the <u>school</u> band play.

6. I won a prize and put it on the <u>shelf</u> under my window.

7. Then Dad treated us to ice cream with <u>chocolate</u> sauce.

Spell Chat
Challenge a classmate to think of three more synonyms for **big**. How about five?

B Word Study: **Related Words**

Write the spelling word that goes with the other two words in each group.

8. hill, mountain, ___

9. water, roadway, ___

10. book, cover, ___

11. sling, cast, ___

12. fix, replace, ___

13. actor, scenery, ___

C Write

Write a sign for a yard sale. Use these words.

huge   age   cage

___

___

Be a Spelling Sleuth

Look at packages for words that end in ge or dge. For example, a food package might say **large size**. A game box might say **for every age**.

Spelling Words

age	ridge
cage	bridge
page	edge
stage	ledge
large	bandage
change	village
budge	college LOOKOUT WORD
fudge	

Review	Challenge
garage	challenge
huge	manage
earn	

My Words

___

___

___

___

Spelling Words

age	ridge
cage	bridge
page	edge
stage	ledge
large	bandage
change	village
budge	college LOOKOUT WORD
fudge	

Review	Challenge
garage	challenge
huge	manage
earn	

My Words

Quick Write

Make up a title for a movie. Use two spelling words that end in **ge** and **dge**.

You may wish to do this activity on a computer.

A Write About a Folk Tale Character

Make up a folk tale character. Tell where the character lives and what happens. Give your folk tale a name. Use as many spelling words as possible.

B Proofread

Yolanda wrote about a folk tale character she invented. She made three spelling errors and one punctuation error. She also forgot to capitalize a word in the title.

Tip

Capitalize the names of people, places, and the main words in story titles.

Flora and the singing Bear
Flora lived at the ege of
a small town. Her best friend
was a lardge brown bear.
One day Flora ran out of food.
She needed to ern some money.
"Let's put on a show for the
village," said Flora to
the bear "I will dance
and you can sing."

PROOFREADING MARKS

∧ Add
⊙ Add a period
ℓ Take out
⌒ Move
≡ Capital letter
／ Small letter
¶ Indent paragraph

Now proofread your story.
Check spelling, punctuation, and capitalization.

A Use the Dictionary: **Pronunciation**

The dictionary shows how to pronounce a word. You'll find the pronunciation after the entry word between slashes. The symbols and letters that show how to spell a word are given in a key in the Spelling Dictionary. Use the pronunciations to help you say these words.

change /chānj/
vil•lage /vil ij/
col•lege /kol ij/

Write the spelling word for each pronunciation.

/pāj/ _____ /stāj/ _____

/fuj/ _____ /brij/ _____

Use the Spelling Dictionary to find the pronunciation for these words. Write what you find.

large _____ ledge _____

B Test Yourself

This may look like a list of nonsense words. However, when you add **ge** or **dge**, you make real words.
Add the correct letters, and write the spelling words.

1. a	**5.** banda	**9.** bu	**13.** lar
2. villa	**6.** bri	**10.** fu	**14.** chan
3. colle	**7.** ca	**11.** e	**15.** sta
4. pa	**8.** le	**12.** ri	

For Tomorrow...
Get ready to share the *ge* and *dge* words you discovered, and remember to study for the test!

Get Word Wise

The words **cage** and **cave** come from the Latin word **cava**, meaning "hollow place." Today, a cage is a home to some small animals. A cave is a hole in the ground.

Word Study Strategy

START

See the word

Say it slowly

Link sounds and letters

Write

Check

END

Words With ch and sh

A See and Say

Spelling Words

chin	shape
check	shark
checkers	shine
chicken	shy
beach	brush
reach	finish
teacher	machine
march	

LOOKOUT WORD

Review	Challenge
college	fashion
kitten	chapter
sheep	

My Words

_____

_____

_____

_____

The Spelling Concept

ch	chin	beach
sh	shark	brush

Two letters can stand for one sound. The letters **ch** stand for /ch/. The letters **sh** stand for /sh/.

Mac Hines fixes **machines**.

MEMORY JOGGER

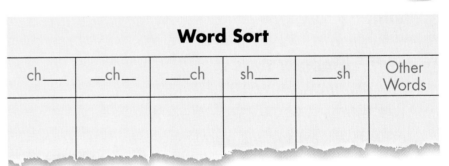

B Link Sounds and Letters

Say each spelling word. Listen for /ch/ or /sh/. Look at each word to see where **ch** or **sh** is. Then sort the spelling words on a chart like this one.

Word Sort

ch___	___ch___	___ch	sh___	___sh	Other Words

C Write and Check

In which words in the riddle do you hear /ch/ or /sh/? Write the two words that are spelling words.

_____

_____

RIDDLE

Why did the chicken buy the cheddar cheese?

She was too short to reach the mozzarella.

A Build Vocabulary: **Word Patterns**

Write the spelling word that goes with each clue.

1. begins with r
2. has the word **arch** in it
3. rhymes with **fine**
4. begins with f
5. rhymes with **deck**
6. ends like **crackers**

Spell Chat
Turn to the person next to you, and challenge him or her to name three places spelled with ch or sh.

B Word Study: **Plurals**

You make most words plural by adding **s**, as in **ships**. You add **es** to words that end with **ch** or **sh**, as in **lunches** and **dishes**. Write the plural of these words.

7. One chin, two ___
8. One brush, two ___
9. One teacher, two ___
10. One chicken, two ___
11. One beach, two ___

12. One shark, two ___
13. One shape, two ___
14. One machine, two ___
15. One kitten, two ___

C Write

Write the first sentence of a newspaper article. Use these spelling words.

shy   sheep

_____

_____

Be a Spelling Sleuth
In the supermarket, look for food words with ch or sh, such as **fish**, **mashed potatoes**, and **chili**. Keep a list.

Spelling Words

chin	shape
check	shark
checkers	shine
chicken	shy
beach	brush
reach	finish
teacher	machine
march	

LOOKOUT WORD

Review	Challenge
college	fashion
kitten	chapter
sheep	

My Words

_____

_____

_____

Spelling Words

chin	shape
check	shark
checkers	shine
chicken	shy
beach	brush
reach	finish
teacher	machine *(LOOKOUT WORD)*
march	

Review	Challenge
college	fashion
kitten	chapter
sheep	

My Words

_____

_____

_____

_____

Quick Write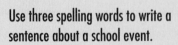

Use three spelling words to write a sentence about a school event.

You may wish to do this activity on a computer.

A Write About an Event

You just marched in a parade with one of your heroes. At 1:15 you rush home to E-mail the news to a friend. Use three spelling words. Tell the time the parade started or finished. Be sure to use a colon between the hour and the minutes.

Tip
When you form plurals, remember to add **es** to words that end in ch or sh.

B Proofread

Angela wrote this E-mail message. She made two spelling errors, one punctuation error, and a mistake in a plural ending. Correct her errors.

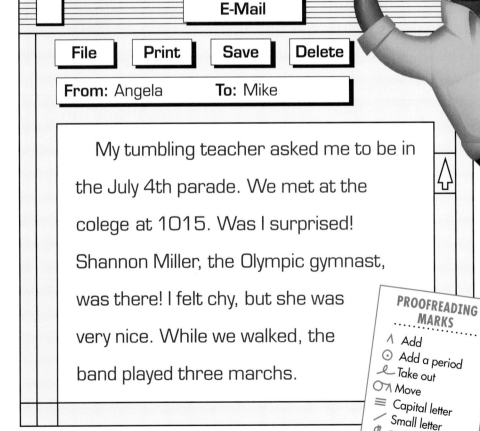

E-Mail

File   Print   Save   Delete

From: Angela   **To:** Mike

My tumbling teacher asked me to be in the July 4th parade. We met at the colege at 1015. Was I surprised! Shannon Miller, the Olympic gymnast, was there! I felt chy, but she was very nice. While we walked, the band played three marchs.

PROOFREADING MARKS

∧ Add
⊙ Add a period
ℓ Take out
↶ Move
≡ Capital letter
/ Small letter
¶ Indent paragraph

Now proofread your paragraph. Check spelling, punctuation, and plurals.

Ⓐ Use the Dictionary: **Parts of Speech**

The dictionary tells what part of speech a word is. Some words can be more than one part of speech. Here is the dictionary entry for **brush**.

> **brush** /brush/
> 1. *noun* An object with bristles and a handle, used for sweeping, painting, or smoothing hair.
> 2. *verb* To use a brush.

Read each sentence. Which part of speech is **brush**?

Be sure to paint with a clean brush. _____

I have to brush my teeth. _____

Write a sentence, using **brush** as a noun. Write another sentence, using **brush** as a verb.

_____

_____

Ⓑ Test Yourself

Write the spelling word that goes with each clue.

1. a barnyard bird
2. works in a school
3. to complete
4. a piece of equipment
5. under your lips
6. used for painting
7. to walk with uniform steps
8. cashed at a bank
9. a game
10. bashful
11. a square or circle
12. a place with sand
13. to polish
14. to stretch for
15. a large fish

For Tomorrow...
Get ready to share the ch and sh words you discovered, and remember to study for your test!

Get Word Wise

Long ago, the Roman year began with the month of **March**. The Romans felt that the beginning of the year was a good time to begin war. So they named this first month after Mars, the god of war. Later, March became the third month, as it is today.

Word Study Strategy

START
See the word
Say it slowly
Link sounds and letters
Write
Check
END

LESSON 17

Spelling Words

coach	itch
couch	match
ranch	watch
bench	stretch
pinch	ditch
punch	pitch
crunch	sandwich
catch	

Review	Challenge
machine	ostrich
season	launch
branches	

My Words

_____

_____

_____

_____

Words That End With ch or tch

A See and Say

The Spelling Concept

ch	ranch	coach
tch	watch	catch

Many words end with /ch/. The /ch/ sound is usually spelled **ch** when it follows a consonant or two vowels. The /ch/ sound is usually spelled **tch** when it follows a short vowel.

B Link Sounds and Letters

Say each spelling word. Listen for the final /ch/. Is it spelled **ch** or **tch**? Sort the spelling words on a chart like this one.

Never put tea in a sandwich!

MEMORY JOGGER

Word Sort

_____ch	_____tch

C Write and Check

How many words with /ch/ can you find in the joke? Write the three that are spelling words.

_____

_____

_____

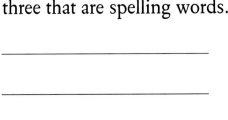

JOKE

What does a ranch hand have for lunch?

a sandwich and cow punch

A Build Vocabulary: **Rhyming Words**

Some words, such as **munch** and **bunch**, rhyme. Read each word, and write the spelling word or words that rhyme with it.

1. word that rhymes with **inch**
2. word that rhymes with **French**
3. word that rhymes with **poach**
4. word that rhymes with **pouch**
5. word that rhymes with **fetch**
6–7. two words that rhyme with **bunch**
8–9. two words that rhyme with **patch**
10–12. three words that rhyme with **switch**

Spell Chat
Turn to a classmate, and say two other words that rhyme with **crunch**.

B Word Study: **Words Ending With -er**

A word that ends in **-er** often means "someone who." For example, someone who can **teach** is a **teacher**. Add **-er** to the underlined words to make new words.

13. someone who works on a <u>ranch</u>
14. someone who can <u>catch</u> a ball
15. someone who can <u>pitch</u> a ball
16. someone who can <u>watch</u>

C Write

Describe a sandwich that might be on a funny menu. Use these spelling words: **sandwich**, **season**.

_____

_____

_____

Be a Spelling Sleuth
Look in newspapers and on sports cards. Find words about sports with ch or tch, such as **coach** and soccer **match**.

Spelling Words

coach	itch
couch	match
ranch	watch
bench	stretch
pinch	ditch
punch	pitch
crunch	sandwich
catch	

LOOKOUT WORD

Review	Challenge
machine	ostrich
season	launch
branches	

My Words

_____

_____

_____

Spelling Words

coach	itch
couch	match
ranch	watch
bench	stretch
pinch	ditch
punch	pitch
crunch	sandwich
catch	

sandwich — LOOKOUT WORD

Review	Challenge
machine	ostrich
season	launch
branches	

My Words

_____

_____

_____

_____

Quick Write

Write a tip on how to eat a messy sandwich. Use three spelling words.

A Write Coaching Tips

You may wish to do this activity on a computer.

Imagine that you are a sports coach at a summer sports camp. Write three tips to help your players do their best. Use at least two spelling words. Be sure to write complete sentences.

B Proofread

Ari wrote three coaching tips. He made three spelling errors, one capitalization error, and wrote one incomplete sentence. Correct his errors.

Tip
A sentence tells a complete thought. It tells who or what, and it tells what happens.

1. a good player keeps an eye on the coatch.

2. A catcher must always wach the ball.

3. Can practice with a batting mashine.

PROOFREADING MARKS

∧ Add
⊙ Add a period
ℓ Take out
↶↗ Move
≡ Capital letter
／ Small letter
¢ Indent paragraph

Now proofread your tips. Check for spelling, capitalization, and complete sentences.

Get Word Wise

Before cars and planes, the fastest way to travel was in coaches pulled by horses. The word **coach** comes from **Kocs (koch)**, a village in Hungary where coaches were first used.

Ⓐ Use the Dictionary: **Idioms**

An idiom is a group of words that means something different from what the words mean one by one. For example, "to pitch in" means "to give help." It has nothing to do with throwing a baseball.

Sometimes an idiom is given as part of a dictionary entry. It usually comes at the end of the entry. Read the entry below, and find the idiom.

> **step** /step/
> 1. *noun* The flat part of a staircase. 2. *verb* To move your legs as in walking. 3. *idiom* If someone says you should "watch your step," the person is telling you to be careful.

Use the idiom in a sentence of your own.

_____

Find an idiom on page 168 in your Spelling Dictionary. Write the idiom and its meaning.

_____

_____

Word Study Strategy

See the word

START

Say it slowly

Link sounds and letters

Write

Check

END

Ⓑ Test Yourself

Write each spelling word with all its letters.

1. pun _
2. pin _
3. coa _
4. cou _
5. mar _
6. wa _
7. ma _
8. di _
9. pi _
10. ben _
11. ran _
12. crun _
13. i _
14. sandwi _
15. stre _

For Tomorrow…
Get ready to share the words ending with ch *and* tch, *and remember to study for your test!*

SHARK!

Fill in the blanks with spelling words from the box.

beach   gentle   large   change   guard

When you say **shark**, most people think the same thing. They picture a (1) fish with sharp teeth. They must (2) against sharks when swimming at an ocean (3) . However, that picture is beginning to (4) . In fact, some sharks are quite (5) and harmless. For example, the whale shark only eats small plants and fish.

age   shape   just   shark   sandwich

There are many different kinds of sharks. Sharks are not all the same size and (6) . The smallest is called the dwarf (7) . It's (8) a foot long—no bigger than a submarine or hero (9) ! Compare that with the largest shark, the whale shark. When a whale shark is about ten years of (10) , it can be 50 feet long!

brush   cage   game   watch   job

People whose (11) it is to study sharks often work in an underwater (12) . That way, they can (13) the sharks safely. Although most people think all sharks are dangerous, many of them are not. Sometimes a shark will (14) up against a diver. That may sound frightening, but with many sharks, it's no more dangerous than a (15) of tag.

Multiple Meanings

Some words have two different meanings. Write the spelling word that has both these meanings.

1. ▪ a word for **look**
   ▪ something that tells time _____

2. ▪ a board game
   ▪ workers at a supermarket _____

3. ▪ make holes in paper
   ▪ a party drink _____

4. ▪ make something different
   ▪ a handful of coins _____

5. ▪ a mark (✓)
   ▪ to see if something is right _____

6. ▪ a game of tennis
   ▪ something that starts a fire _____

7. ▪ a fairy tale character
   ▪ very large in size _____

change
check
giant
punch
match
watch
checkers

Word Associations

ranch   crunch   chin
catch   teacher

Read the two words. Write the spelling word they make you think of.

8. toss, ball, _____

9. eyes, nose, _____

10. horses, cowhand, _____

11. munch, crackle, _____

12. student, school, _____

Mystery Word

- This word is made up of two small words.

- The first word names a group of musicians.

- The second word means how old you are.

  What's the word?

  _____

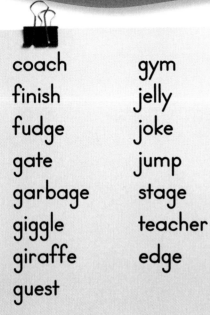

coach   gym

finish   jelly

fudge   joke

gate   jump

garbage   stage

giggle   teacher

giraffe   edge

guest

Tip
Remember that /j/ can be spelled with **g**.

PROOFREADING MARKS

∧ Add
⊙ Add a period
ℓ Take out
↶ Move
≡ Capital letter
／ Small letter
¶ Indent paragraph

Spread the News

Flyers are one way to tell about an event. For example, **Brush up on your game of checkers at noon tomorrow.** Write a sentence or two for a flyer about each event. Use two or more spelling words.

1. A community clean-up day

_____

2. A visitor who will speak at your school

_____

3. A contest for funny stories

_____

4. A food sale to help the school library

_____

5. A sports day

_____

Look back at My Words and the words you misspelled in your Unit 3 Posttests. Use them to write another sentence for a flyer.

6. A school trip

_____

Broadcast It

Choose one of the events above and write a radio announcement for it. Proofread for spelling, capitalization, and punctuation. Then read it to a partner.

_____

_____

Word Clues

The letter **g** can have more than one sound, /g/ or /j/. Write the spelling word with the letter **g** that goes with each clue.

> garbage   large   garden
> giraffe   age   geese

1. This animal sticks its neck out. _____

2. These animals honk and fly. _____

3. This is not small. _____

4. This is something you throw away. _____

5. This is a place where you dig in the dirt. _____

6. This tells how old someone is. _____

> page   village   gave
> giggle   garage   gym

7. This is a small town. _____

8. This is a place where you play games. _____

9. This is something you find in a book. _____

10. This is where you find cars and trucks. _____

11. This is a real chuckle. _____

Lisa says...

I once wrote a news story about the new gym at our school. In my first draft, I wrote **j-i-m** instead of **g-y-m**. My friend Amy read it, and asked, "Who's the new kid named Jim?"

At first I didn't know what my friend was talking about. Then it hit me. I had written the wrong word! I forgot that /j/ can be spelled with the letter **g**. I should have written **gym**!

Spelling Matters!

Spelling Words

oil	choice
boil	voice
soil	boy
spoil	joy
join	toy
point	enjoy
poison	royal LOOKOUT WORD
noise	

Review	Challenge
sandwich	oyster
croak	loyalty
float	

My Words

Words With oi or oy

A See and Say

The Spelling Concept

oi	oil	noise
oy	toy	enjoy

The letters **oi** and **oy** stand for /oi/. You will usually find **oi** in the middle of words and **oy** at the end of words.

Be cool! Think **ice** to spell cho**ice** and vo**ice**.

MEMORY JOGGER

B Link Sounds and Letters

Say each spelling word. Listen for /oi/. Look at each word to see where **oi** or **oy** is. Then sort the spelling words on a chart like this one.

Word Sort

oi__	__oi__	__oy__	__oy

C Write and Check

In which words in the Brain Teaser do you hear /oi/? Write the two that are spelling words.

_____

_____

BRAIN TEASER
What's the fastest way to make oil boil?

Add the letter b!

Vocabulary Practice

Ⓐ Build Vocabulary: **Action Verbs**

An action verb tells what a person or thing does. **Play** and **read** are action verbs. Write an action verb from your spelling list that answers each question.

What do you do. . .

1. with a squeaky door?
   You _____ it.

2. with a raw potato?
   You _____ it.

3. with your favorite toy?
   You _____ it.

4. if you put salt on ice cream?
   You _____ it.

5. to be a member of a group?
   You _____ it.

Spell Chat
Ask the person next to you another question that can be answered by using an action verb with /oi/.

Ⓑ Word Study: **Relationships**

Write a spelling word that goes with each pair of words.

6. loud, crash, ___
7. tip, end, ___
8. smile, happiness, ___
9. harmful, dangerous, ___
10. dirt, earth, ___
11. crown, queen, ___
12. game, doll, ___
13. speak, talk, ___
14. choose, pick, ___
15. brother, child, ___

Ⓒ Write

Write a sentence that tells about something you like to do. Use these words.

enjoy   float

_____

_____

Spelling Words

oil	choice
boil	voice
soil	boy
spoil	joy
join	toy
point	enjoy
poison	royal
noise	

Review	Challenge
sandwich	oyster
croak	loyalty
float	

My Words

_____

_____

_____

_____

Spelling Words

oil	choice
boil	voice
soil	boy
spoil	joy
join	toy
point	enjoy
poison	royal *LOOKOUT WORD*
noise	

Review	Challenge
sandwich	oyster
croak	loyalty
float	

My Words

_____

_____

_____

_____

Quick Write

Write two sentences about a toy you would like to have. Use spelling words with /oi/.

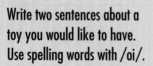

You may wish to do this activity on a computer.

A Write a Description

Invent a toy that you might see in a cartoon. Name it and tell what it can do. Use three spelling words and some exciting action verbs. Be sure the subject and verb in each sentence agree in number.

B Proofread

Pat wrote about an animated toy. She made three spelling errors, one punctuation error, and one error in subject-verb agreement. Correct the errors.

Spelling Tip
Remember that /oi/ at the end of a word will usually be spelled oy.

Lloyd has a shiny, metal robot named Troy. Troy talks in a low, rough voyce. He can click, buzz, and croke as he moves Sometimes he like to join the kids for a swim in the lake. Then Lloyd has to oyl Troy's joints.

PROOFREADING MARKS

∧ Add
⊙ Add a period
ℓ Take out
↻⤴ Move
≡ Capital letter
∕ Small letter
¢ Indent paragraph

Now proofread your description. Check for spelling, punctuation, and subject-verb agreement.

A Use the Dictionary: Guide Words

Guide words at the top of each dictionary page help you find words on that page. The guide words are the first and last entry words on the page. Remember that entry words are in alphabetical order.

> pie • rang
>
> **point** /point/
>
> 1. *verb* To show where something is by using your index finger
> 2. *noun* The sharp end of something, as in a *pencil point*.

Write the spelling word or words you would find on the same page with the following guide words. Check your work in the Spelling Dictionary.

check • contest _____   trap • wash _____

blink • can't   _____   spend • store _____

jelly • keep   _____   rather • rung _____

B Test Yourself

Which spelling word do you think of when you read each word or phrase below? Write the word.

1. loud sounds
2. young man
3. dirt
4. king
5. plaything
6. talk
7. grease
8. dot
9. happiness
10. harmful
11. fasten together
12. like to do
13. ruin
14. your pick
15. cook

> *For Tomorrow...*
> Get ready to share the *oi* and *oy* words you discovered, and remember to study for your test!

Get Word Wise

The word **boil** comes from the Latin word **bulla**, meaning "bubble." What do you see as a liquid boils? You see bubbles that rise to the top.

Word Study Strategy

See the word

START

Say it slowly

Link sounds and letters

Write

Check

END

Same Sound, Different Letters

Ⓐ See and Say

Spelling Words

bird	turtle
girl	purple
first	word
circle	work
circus	worm
hurt	world
turn	were **LOOKOUT WORD**
nurse	

Review	Challenge
royal	furniture
giraffe	thirsty
Thursday	

My Words

The Spelling Concept

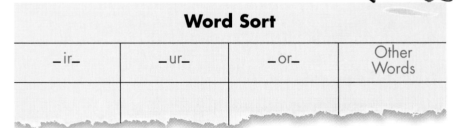

ir	bird
ur	nurse
or	word

Sometimes different letters can stand for the same sound. The letters **ir**, **ur**, and **or** can all stand for /ûr/.

> You were where? Here or there?

MEMORY JOGGER

Ⓑ Link Sounds and Letters

Say each spelling word. Look at the way /ûr/ is spelled. Sort your spelling words on a chart like this one. Make a special place for the extra word.

Word Sort

_ir_	_ur_	_or_	Other Words

Ⓒ Write and Check

Read the joke. Find three spelling words and write them on the lines.

_____

_____

_____

JOKE
Why did the early bird look like a grape?

It ate a purple worm.

Ⓐ Build Vocabulary: **Letter Patterns**

Some words that rhyme are spelled with the same ending letters. Other words that rhyme are spelled with different ending letters. Write the spelling word that rhymes with each of these words.

1. shirt
2. churn
3. thirst

4. fur
5. jerk
6. germ

Spell Chat
Challenge a classmate to think of four number words with /ûr/, such as **first**.

Ⓑ Word Study: **Pronouns**

Pronouns are words that take the place of nouns. Solve each riddle by writing the spelling word that takes the place of the underlined pronoun.

7. <u>It</u> has feathers. What is <u>it</u>?

8. <u>It</u> is something you say. What is <u>it</u>?

9. <u>It</u> is not a square. What is <u>it</u>?

10. <u>She</u> is a child. Who is <u>she</u>?

11. <u>It</u> has a hard shell. What is <u>it</u>?

12. <u>It</u> has lots of clowns. What is <u>it</u>?

13. <u>It</u> is the Earth. What is <u>it</u>?

14. <u>He</u> works with a doctor. Who is <u>he</u>?

15. <u>It</u> is a color. What is <u>it</u>?

Ⓒ Write

Write the first sentence of a story. Use these words.

girl   giraffe   purple   Thursday

_____

_____

Be a Spelling Sleuth
On your way to and from school, look for signs that have /ûr/ words such as **turn** and **thirty**. Keep a list.

Spelling Words

bird	turtle
girl	purple
first	word
circle	work
circus	worm
hurt	world
turn	were
nurse	

Review	Challenge
royal	furniture
giraffe	thirsty
Thursday	

My Words

_____

_____

_____

_____

Spelling Words

bird	turtle
girl	purple
first	word
circle	work
circus	worm
hurt	world
turn	were
nurse	

were — LOOKOUT WORD

Review	Challenge
royal	furniture
giraffe	thirsty
Thursday	

My Words

_____

_____

_____

Quick Write

Suppose that you have wriggled into a "worm circus." Write one sentence that describes a trick the worms do. Use at least two spelling words.

A Write a Note

You may wish to do this activity on a computer.

You have just been to a terrific circus. Write a note telling a friend about it. Describe something about the sights and sounds. Use three spelling words.

B Proofread

Anita wrote this note to a friend. She made three spelling errors and one capitalization error. She also used one noun twice. She needs to use a pronoun in its place the second time. Correct Anita's errors.

Tip
Remember that you can use a pronoun in place of a noun.

April 10

Dear Aaron,

last Thersday, Ms. Rose took me to my first circus. I saw the best acrobats in the whole wurld. The acrobats made a people pyramid. A cool clown with pirpl hair was so-o-o funny. It was a great show!

Your friend,
Anita

Now proofread your note. Check for spelling and capitalization and the correct use of pronouns.

PROOFREADING MARKS

∧ Add
⊙ Add a period
ℓ Take out
↶↷ Move
≡ Capital letter
／ Small letter
¶ Indent paragraph

Ⓐ Use the Dictionary: Multiple Meanings

Some words have more than one meaning. In a
dictionary, the different meanings are numbered.
Here are the meanings for **word**.

> **word** /wûrd/ *noun*
> 1. a unit of spoken sounds or letters that has a
> meaning 2. a remark or comment
> 3. a short conversation 4. a promise

Which meaning fits the way **word** is used in each
sentence? Write the number before the sentence.

_____ Ms. Brown gave Brandon a word of advice.

_____ Tina gave her word she would clean her room.

_____ I used the word in a sentence.

Write your own sentence, using **word** to mean "a short
conversation."

_____

Ⓑ Test Yourself

The vowel + **r** is missing from each spelling word below.
Think of the missing letters and write each complete word.

1. h _ t	5. f _ st	9. w _ k	13. g _ l
2. b _ d	6. w _ m	10. t _ n	14. n _ se
3. w _ ld	7. t _ tle	11. w _ d	15. c _ cus
4. p _ ple	8. c _ cle	12. w _ e	

For Tomorrow...
Get ready to share found
words with /ûr/, and remember
to study for your test!

Get Word Wise

Circle and **circus** both come from
the Latin word **circus**, which means
"ring." Originally a **circus**
was any kind of
entertainment
that took
place in a
round area.

**Word Study
Strategy**

START

See the word

Say it slowly

Link sounds and letters

Write

Check

END

Spelling Words

for
four 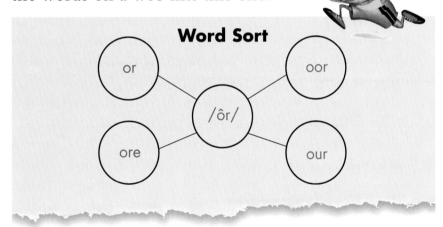 *LOOKOUT WORD*
before
forest
born
corner
morning
storm

porch
orange
door
floor
more
store
wore

Review	Challenge
were	orchestra
guard	chorus
story	

My Words

_____

_____

_____

Words With the Sound of **or**

Ⓐ See and Say

The Spelling Concept

or	born	oor	door
our	four	ore	store

The sound /ôr/ can be spelled **or, our, oor,** and **ore.**

Ⓑ Link Sounds and Letters

Say each spelling word. Look at the way /ôr/ is spelled in each word. Then sort the words on a web like this one.

Do you like the color orange?

MEMORY JOGGER

Word Sort

or — /ôr/ — oor

ore — /ôr/ — our

Ⓒ Write and Check

1. Start with **more**.
2. Change **e** to **n**.
3. Add **-ing**.

1. _____

2. _____

3. _____

ANSWER THIS!
What comes after night and before noon?

(Follow the directions to get the answer.)

A Build Vocabulary: **Opposites**

Opposites are words that are as different as **sweet** and **sour**. Read each word. Then write the spelling word that is the opposite.

1. evening
2. ceiling
3. less
4. after
5. died

Spell Chat
Challenge the person next to you to think of another pair of opposites with the sound of or.

B Word Study: **Nouns**

A **noun** is a word that names a person, place, or thing. Play the game I Spy by writing the noun that the adjectives describe. The answer will be a Spelling Word or a Review Word.

I spy…

6. a sweet, juicy _____
7. a squeaky, swinging _____
8. a leafy, cool _____
9. a loud lightning _____
10. a crowded grocery _____
11. a breezy front _____
12. an exciting adventure _____
13. a busy street _____

C Write

Write a sentence that tells how someone was dressed for a costume party. Use the words **wore, four** and **for**.

_____

_____

_____

Be a Spelling Sleuth
Look at ads and posters for words with the sound of or. Keep a list.

Spelling Words

for	porch
four	orange
before	door
forest	floor
born	more
corner	store
morning	wore
storm	

LOOKOUT WORD

Review	Challenge
were	orchestra
guard	chorus
story	

My Words

_____

_____

_____

_____

Spelling Words

for
four LOOKOUT WORD
before
forest
born
corner
morning
storm

porch
orange
door
floor
more
store
wore

Review	Challenge
were	orchestra
guard	chorus
story	

My Words

_____

_____

_____

_____

Quick Write

Write a sentence telling something you might do to prepare for a big storm. Use two spelling words.

You may wish to do this activity on a computer.

Ⓐ Write a Story

Imagine you are a TV weatherperson. Write a news story about a big storm. Give details about what's happening. Use three spelling words in your story.

Ⓑ Proofread

Mark wrote this news story about a snowstorm. He made three spelling errors, one punctuation error, and one capitalization error. Correct the errors.

Tip
Remember to use a period or question mark at the end of every sentence.

What's the big storey this morning A winter storm has dropped eight inches of snow in fore hours. Many schools, offices, and stores are closed. cars are stuck at corners. If you're going out the dore, be sure to take your skis along. More later.

Now proofread your news story. Check for spelling, punctuation, and capitalization.

PROOFREADING MARKS

∧ Add
⊙ Add a period
ℓ Take out
○↗ Move
≡ Capital letter
/ Small letter
¶ Indent paragraph

Ⓐ Use the Dictionary: **Definitions**

People look up words in the dictionary for
different reasons. Often they use a dictionary
to find out what a word means. This entry gives three
meanings for the word **store**.

> **store** /stôr/
> 1. *noun* A place where things are sold. 2. *noun* A
> supply or stock of something. 3. *verb* To put things
> away until they are needed. ▷ **storing, stored**

Get Word Wise

The word **forest** comes from the
Latin word **foris**, which means
"outside." A woodland, or forest,
was always "outside" a town.
From this word we get our
word **forest**.

Read these definitions and write the spelling word
that has that meaning.

Where two sides of something meet. _____

The number between three and five. _____

A color made by mixing yellow and red. _____

Ⓑ Test Yourself

These spelling words are missing all their vowels.
Fill in the vowels and write the words.

1. c _ rn _ r
2. d _ _ r
3. b _ f _ r _
4. b _ rn
5. st _ r _
6. f _ r
7. _ r _ ng _
8. st _ rm

9. f _ _ r
10. w _ r _
11. m _ r _
12. m _ rn _ ng
13. f _ r _ st
14. fl _ _ r
15. p _ rch

For Tomorrow...
Get ready to share the
/ôr/ words that you
discovered, and
remember to study
for your test!

**Word Study
Strategy**

START

See the word

Say
it slowly

Link
sounds
and
letters

Write

Check

END

Learn and Spell

Spelling Words

cool	loose
fool	lose **LOOKOUT WORD**
roof	choose
noon	flute
balloon	rude
cocoon	mule
goose	music
moose	

Review	Challenge
four	shampoo
fudge	kangaroo
glue	

My Words

_____

_____

_____

_____

Words With the Vowel Sounds in cool and music

A See and Say

The Spelling Concept

cool	music
flute	mule

The vowel sound in **cool** can be spelled **oo** as in **noon** or **u**-consonant-**e** as in **flute**. The vowel sound in **music** can be spelled **u** or **u**-consonant-**e** as in **mule**.

Oops! The goose is loose.

MEMORY JOGGER

B Link Sounds and Letters

Read each spelling word. Say each word and listen for the vowel sounds in **cool** and **music**. Then sort the spelling words on a chart like this.

Word Sort

Words with /o͞o/		Words with /yo͞o/	
oo as in cool	Other Words	u as in music	Other Words

C Write and Check

Write the words in Rhyme Time that have the vowel sound in **fool**.

_____

_____

RHYME TIME
What do you call a cold swimming hole?

a cool pool

A Build Vocabulary: **Rhyming Words**

Read the word at the top of each set. Write the spelling words that rhyme with it. Remember that the vowel sounds in words are sometimes spelled differently.

tool

1. _____
2. _____

caboose

5. _____
6. _____
7. _____

cocoon

3. _____
4. _____

whose

8. _____
9. _____

Spell Chat
Challenge a partner to think of another rhyme for **tool, moon, caboose,** and **whose.**

B Word Study: **Related Words**

Write a spelling word to complete each group of words below.

10. horse, donkey, _____
11. butterfly, caterpillar, _____
12. song, melody, _____
13. house, attic, _____
14. nasty, mean, _____
15. violin, trumpet, _____

C Write

Write a funny sentence about a goose and a balloon.

_____

_____

Spelling Words

cool
fool
roof
noon
balloon
cocoon
goose
moose

loose
lose
choose
flute
rude
mule
music

LOOKOUT WORD

Review	Challenge
four	shampoo
fudge	kangaroo
glue	

My Words

_____

_____

_____

Spelling Words

cool
fool
roof
noon
balloon
cocoon
goose
moose

loose
lose — LOOKOUT WORD
choose
flute
rude
mule
music

Review	Challenge
four	shampoo
fudge	kangaroo
glue	

My Words

_____

_____

_____

_____

Quick Write

Write a title for a mystery.
Use two spelling words.

A **Write a Mystery Story**   You may wish to do this activity on a computer.

In some mysteries, an object is lost and then found.
A mystery title can give you clues about what happens.
Write about what might happen in a mystery called
"Mr. Toon's Missing Balloon." Use two spelling words.

B **Proofread**

Gloria wrote a mystery story
called "A Flute on the Loose."
She made three spelling errors,
one punctuation error, and one
capitalization error. Correct them.

Tip

Add **'s** to a noun to
show ownership.
For example,
Jake's goose.

Where was Bruces flute?
How could he loose it?
He had last played it
fore days ago. Outside, his
sisters were having a yard
sale. Suddenly, bruce heard
moosic. A girl was playing
his flute. It wasn't lost.
It was for sale!

PROOFREADING MARKS

∧ Add
⊙ Add a period
ℓ Take out
↶↷ Move
≡ Capital letter
╱ Small letter
¶ Indent paragraph

Now proofread your mystery.
Check for spelling, punctuation, and
capital letters. Make sure you add **'s** to nouns
that show ownership.

A Use the Thesaurus: **Synonyms**

A thesaurus is a dictionary of synonyms.
The entry words are in alphabetical order. Each entry word is followed by other words that have the same or almost the same meaning. Read the thesaurus entries.

choose *verb* pick, select
- You could *choose* to drink milk or juice.
- Danny will *pick* his favorite toy to bring along.
- She may *select* crayons or markers to draw with.

rude *adjective* impolite
- It is rude not to say "Thank you."
- Talking when someone else is speaking is *impolite*.

Write a synonym for each underlined word.

His <u>rude</u> answer shocked everyone! _____

You may <u>choose</u> a video to watch today. _____

B Test Yourself

The spelling words are missing their vowels.
Write each word correctly.

1. m _ l _
2. ch _ _ s _
3. n _ _ n
4. r _ d _
5. b _ ll _ _ n

6. c _ _ l
7. m _ s _ c
8. g _ _ s _
9. m _ _ s _
10. r _ _ f

11. c _ c _ _ n
12. fl _ t _
13. f _ _ l
14. l _ s _
15. l _ _ s _

For Tomorrow...
Get ready to share the words with the vowel sounds in *cool* and *music* that you discovered. Remember to study for your test!

Get Word Wise
The **moose** got its name from a Native American tribe, the Algonquins, that lived in the eastern United States. The Algonquin word **mus** means "he strips off the bark." That's exactly what a moose does when it eats its dinner!

Word Study Strategy

See the word

START

Say it slowly

Link sounds and letters

Write

Check

END

Spelling Words

care	chair
dare	fair
scare	fairy
share	hair
stare	pair
parents	stairs
air	their LOOKOUT WORD
airplane	

Review	Challenge
lose	everywhere
march	square
afraid	

My Words

_____

_____

_____

Words With the Sound of air

Ⓐ See and Say

The Spelling Concept

dare	share
airplane	chair

The sound /âr/ is usually spelled **are** or **air**.

> Remember **the** in **their**.
>
> MEMORY JOGGER

Ⓑ Link Sounds and Letters

Say each spelling word. Notice that they all have /âr/. Look at how /âr/ is spelled. Then sort the words on a chart like this one.

Word Sort

are	air	Other Words

Ⓒ Write and Check

Which words rhyme? Write them.

_____

_____

_____

_____

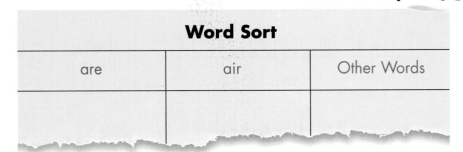

A FAIR DARE

When you go to the fair,
Do you dare
Sit in a chair
That zooms through
the air?

Ⓐ Build Vocabulary: **Homophones**

Homophones are words that sound alike, but their spellings and meanings are different. Write the spelling word that is a homophone for each of the underlined words.

1. What's the <u>fare</u> for the bus?

2. A jack rabbit is a <u>hare</u>.

3. I like to <u>pare</u> an apple before I eat it.

4. My cat <u>stares</u> out the window.

5. <u>There</u> goes the train!

Spell Chat
Challenge a classmate to think of another homophone for **their** and **there**.

Ⓑ Word Study: **Letters and Sounds**

Change the underlined vowels in each word to make a Spelling Word or a Review Word.

6. st<u>o</u>re

7. c<u>u</u>re

8. sh<u>o</u>re

9. ch<u>ee</u>r

10. sc<u>o</u>re

11. <u>ea</u>r

12. f<u>ie</u>ry

13. d<u>i</u>re

14. l<u>ea</u>se

Ⓒ Write

Write two sentences. Use one of these words in each sentence.

airplane   parents

_____

_____

_____

Be a Spelling Sleuth
When reading stories this week, jot down all the words you find that have the sound of air, as in **fair**.

Spelling Words

care	chair
dare	fair
scare	fairy
share	hair
stare	pair
parents	stairs
air	their
airplane	

Review	Challenge
lose	everywhere
march	square
afraid	

My Words

_____

_____

_____

Spelling Words

care   chair
dare   fair
scare   fairy
share   hair
stare   pair
parents   stairs
air   their   LOOKOUT WORD
airplane

Review	Challenge
lose	everywhere
march	square
afraid	

My Words

_____

_____

_____

_____

Quick Write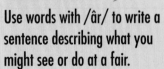

Use words with /âr/ to write a sentence describing what you might see or do at a fair.

A Write a Description

You may wish to do this activity on a computer.

Imagine that you're on an airplane coming home from a trip. Write a postcard to a friend. Tell where you went and what you saw and did. Use at least two spelling words.

Tip
In a compound sentence, always place a comma before the word **or**, **and**, or **but**.

B Proofread

Kate wrote this postcard to a friend. She made three spelling errors, one punctuation error, and one capitalization error. Correct them.

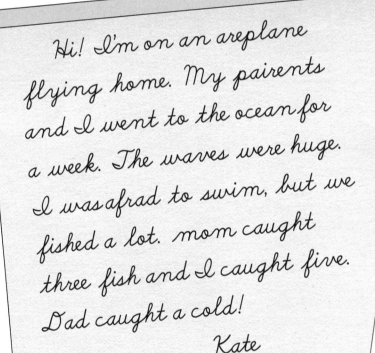

Hi! I'm on an areplane flying home. My pairents and I went to the ocean for a week. The waves were huge. I was afrad to swim, but we fished a lot. mom caught three fish and I caught five. Dad caught a cold!

Kate

PROOFREADING MARKS
∧ Add
⊙ Add a period
ℓ Take out
⌒ Move
≡ Capital letter
／ Small letter
¶ Indent paragraph

Now proofread your postcard. Check for spelling, punctuation, and capitalization.

A Use the Dictionary: **Pronunciation**

Every entry word in the dictionary is followed by a respelling of the word. The letters and symbols tell you how to pronounce the word. This is how the pronunciation for **airplane** is shown.

air•plane /âr plān**/**

Write the spelling word for each of the following dictionary respellings. Use the pronunciation key in your Spelling Dictionary to help you pronounce the letters and symbols in the respelling.

/dâr/ _____   /châr/ _____

/skâr/ _____   /kâr/ _____

/fâr ē/ _____   /shâr/ _____

B Test Yourself

Write a spelling word that means about the same thing as each word or phrase below.

1. to frighten
2. to use together
3. mom and dad
4. what we breathe
5. to challenge
6. two things
7. a character in a story
8. to look for a long time

9. a jet
10. belonging to them
11. grows on the head
12. a seat
13. a festival
14. steps
15. be interested in

For Tomorrow...
Get ready to share the /âr/ words that you discovered, and remember to study for your test!

Get Word Wise
The word **share** is related to the word **shears**, another name for scissors. Both words come from an old English word that meant "to cut." Think about how you might divide something you **share**, like an apple or a sandwich. You could cut it.

Word Study Strategy

See the word

START

Say it slowly

Link sounds and letters

Write

Check

END

Lighter Than Air

Write spelling words from the box to complete the sentences.

> parents   fair   dare   balloon   first

I could hardly believe it. I was about to take my (1) ride in a hot-air (2) . When we got to the (3) , I still wasn't sure I would (4) to go up. Of course, I wasn't going to admit that to my (5) .

> choose   were   orange   choice   their

The balloons (6) every color of the rainbow. We could (7) the balloon we wanted to go up in. Our (8) was a green and (9) one. My parents were as excited as I was. It was (10) first balloon ride, too.

> enjoy   share   airplane   forest   four

All (11) of us—Mom, Dad, the pilot, and me— climbed into the basket. Then the balloon lifted off the ground. A balloon stays closer to the ground than an (12) does. We could just relax and (13) the sights. We floated over the river, a pine (14) , cornfields, and some cows. I took lots of pictures so I could (15) what I saw with my friends. I hope they can all take balloon rides, too. There's nothing more exciting than being lighter than air!

Opposites

Look at the underlined word in each sentence.
Write the spelling word that means the opposite.

first

cool

before

loose

morning

work

1. a very <u>hot</u> day _____

2. the <u>last</u> day of third grade _____

3. <u>play</u> together all afternoon _____

4. a dark, rainy <u>night</u> _____

5. a week <u>after</u> my birthday _____

6. a <u>tight</u> coat _____

Relationships

airplane

brush

balloon

chair

cocoon

beach

Read each set of words. Notice how the first two
words go together. Then choose the spelling word that
completes the second set.

7. knife and fork, comb and _____

8. chicken and egg, butterfly and _____

9. trees and forest, sand and _____

10. water and boat, air and hot-air _____

11. salt and pepper, table and _____

12. car and truck, helicopter and _____

Word Math

Do the word math to find
the answer to the riddle.

more−m−e + range−r =

_____

What grows on a tree, is
round, and flies?

Super _____

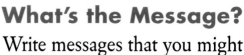

Lesson 24 Review

choose	music
circus	pair
corner	parents
enjoy	porch
flute	purple
four	store
moose	storm
more	turtle

Tip
Remember to end each sentence with the correct punctuation.

What's the Message?

Write messages that you might send to friends on postcards. For example, **My parents and I went to the greatest circus ever!** Use at least two spelling words in each message.

1. You took a hike in the woods.

_____

2. There was a hurricane.

_____

3. You went to a big parade.

_____

4. A new shop opened on your block.

_____

5. You went to a theme park.

_____

Look back at My Words and the words you misspelled in your Unit 4 Posttests. Use them in another message.

6. You went to a fantastic new museum.

_____

Record It

In a short journal entry, tell more about one of the events. Proofread your journal entry for spelling, capitalization, and punctuation.

PROOFREADING MARKS

∧ Add
⊙ Add a period
ℓ Take out
ᵔ Move
≡ Capital letter
/ Small letter
¢ Indent paragraph

_____

_____

Rhyme Time

Read each clue. Then write the spelling word that rhymes. For example, a rhyme for **a chubby lion** is **a fat cat**.

> moose   cool   chair   royal   storm

1. a seat for a grizzly   **a bear** _____

2. rain on a hot day   **a warm** _____

3. a chilly place for swimming   **a** _____ **pool**

4. a drink named after a forest animal   _____ **juice**

5. the land where a queen walks   _____ **soil**

> noon   flute   store   world   noise

6. a globe that was spun around   **a twirled** _____

7. a place that sells something you walk on

   a floor _____

8. a concert of musical wind instruments

   a _____ **toot**

9. the loud sound a drum makes   **a toy's** _____

10. a song at 12 o'clock   **a** _____ **tune**

Howard says...

Last week I was writing a report for science on my computer. In it I wrote, **Moos eat leaves, twigs, and the bark of some woody plants.**

My little sister was reading over my shoulder. "I thought cows just eat grass!" she said. I didn't know what she was talking about, because my report was about **moose**. Then I saw that I misspelled **moose**. Leaving out one letter can really change the meaning of a word!

Spelling Matters!

Consonant Blends With l

A See and Say

The Spelling Concept

black   **fl**ower   **pl**an
cloud   **gl**ass   **sl**ow

A consonant blend is two or three consonants written together. The letter **l** is part of several blends: **bl, cl, fl, gl, pl, sl, spl.**

We saw a flower.

MEMORY
JOGGER

Spelling Words

black	gloves
blame	plain
cloud	plan
club	plant
flower	slide
flight	slow
flash	splash *LOOKOUT WORD*
glass	

Review	Challenge
their	plastic
crunch	sunglasses
play	

My Words

_____

_____

_____

_____

B Link Sounds and Letters

Say each spelling word. Which consonant blend with l do you hear? Sort the spelling words on a chart like this one.

Word Sort

bl	cl	fl	gl	pl	sl	spl

C Write and Check

Find the words in the joke that have a consonant blend with l. Write one spelling word that begins with each of the same consonant blends.

JOKE
Why did the boy take his clock on the plane?

He wanted to see time fly!

_____

_____

_____

Ⓐ Build Vocabulary: **Rhyming Words**

Read each word. Write one spelling word that rhymes with it.

1. light
2. loud
3. loves
4. slash
5. shower
6. ant

7. clash
8. glide
9. flame
10. tan
11. rub

Spell Chat
Challenge a classmate to name an adjective that starts with a consonant blend with l.

Ⓑ Word Study: **Adjectives**

An adjective is a word that describes a noun. Read each sentence. Write the adjective from your spelling list that could take the place of the phrase in ( ).

12. Today I took my lunch in a (not fancy) paper bag.

13. I stood in a (not fast) line to buy milk.

14. I ate my sandwich by a clear (not wood) door.

15. I watched a (not white) cloud roll by.

Ⓒ Write

Write a newspaper headline, using three of the spelling words.

_____

_____

Be a Spelling Sleuth
Check signs in stores and malls. Look for words with consonant blends with l, such as **Plants** and **Caution: Slippery Floor**.

Spelling Words

black	gloves
blame	plain
cloud	plan
club	plant
flower	slide
flight	slow
flash	splash
glass	

LOOKOUT WORD

Review	Challenge
their	plastic
crunch	sunglasses
play	

My Words

_____

_____

_____

Spelling Words

black	gloves
blame	plain
cloud	plan
club	plant
flower	slide
flight	slow
flash	splash LOOKOUT WORD
glass	

Review	Challenge
their	plastic
crunch	sunglasses
play	

My Words

Quick Write

Write an ad for a community get-together. Use three spelling words that have a consonant blend with l.

 You may wish to do this activity on a computer.

A Write a Flyer

Your school has just started a club. Write a flyer describing what the club does and when it meets. Persuade others to join. Use three spelling words.

B Proofread

Pat wrote a flyer about the school's garden club. She made three spelling errors, one punctuation error, and forgot one capital letter. Correct the errors.

Tip
Remember to capitalize names of months and days of the week.

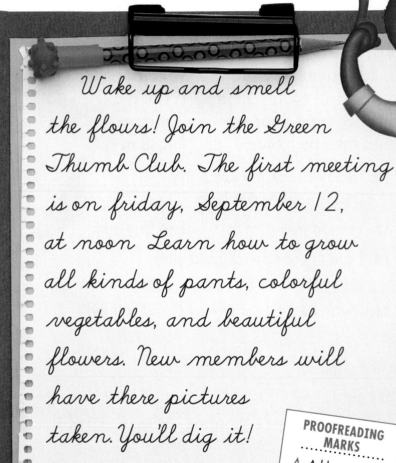

> Wake up and smell the flours! Join the Green Thumb Club. The first meeting is on friday, September 12, at noon Learn how to grow all kinds of pants, colorful vegetables, and beautiful flowers. New members will have there pictures taken. You'll dig it!

PROOFREADING MARKS

∧ Add
⊙ Add a period
ℓ Take out
ᴏᴧ Move
≡ Capital letter
/ Small letter
¶ Indent paragraph

Now proofread your flyer. Check for spelling, punctuation, and capitalization.

A Use the Dictionary: **Homophones**

Homophones are words that sound alike but have different spellings and meanings. When an entry word is a homophone, a dictionary sometimes lists the other word that sounds the same. Here are dictionary entries for the homophones **plain** and **plane**.

> **plain** /plān/ *adjective*
> Simple or not fancy, as in *plain food* or *plain dress*.
> **Plain** sounds like **plane**.

> **plane** /plān/ *noun*
> A machine with wings that flies through the air.
> **Plane** is short for **airplane**.
> **Plane** sounds like **plain**.

Write the correct homophone to complete each sentence. Use the definitions to help you.

The _____ flew across the ocean.

I sat on a _____ wooden chair.

B Test Yourself

Use this code to write your spelling words.

$=pl   #=bl   &=cl   @=gl   *=spl   •=fl   ?=sl   Δ=vowel

1. *Δsh
2. #Δck
3. ?Δw
4. &ΔΔd
5. •Δsh
6. @ΔvΔ
7. $Δn
8. ?Δde
9. #ΔmΔ
10. $Δnt
11. @Δss
12. &Δb
13. •Δwer
14. $ΔΔn
15. •Δght

For Tomorrow...
Get ready to share the words you discovered that begin with consonant blends with l. Remember to study for your test!

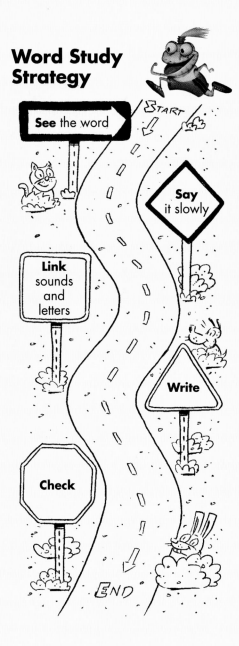

Word Study Strategy

START

See the word

Say it slowly

Link sounds and letters

Write

Check

END

Spelling Words

breeze   front
brain   grand
crab   ground
cross   print
drift   program
drive   trap
frighten   trash
friend *LOOKOUT WORD*

Review	Challenge
splash	tremendous
spoil	grouchy
brave	

My Words

_____

_____

_____

_____

Consonant Blends With r

A See and Say

The Spelling Concept

breeze	crab	drive	friend
grand	print	trap	

The sounds of the letters in a consonant blend are blended together. The letter **r** is part of these blends: **br, cr, dr, fr, gr, pr, tr.**

> Remember the **i** in friend. I am a fri**end** to the **end**!
>
> MEMORY JOGGER

B Link Sounds and Letters

Say each spelling word. Listen for consonant blends with **r**. Look at each word to find the two consonants blended together. Sort the spelling words on a chart like this one.

Word Sort

br	cr	dr	fr	gr	pr	tr

C Write and Check

Find the six consonant blends with **r** that are in this riddle. Write the two that are spelling words.

_____

_____

RIDDLE

What did my friend get when he tried to cross a trumpet with a grape?

a tooty-fruity

Ⓐ Build Vocabulary: **Synonyms**

A synonym is a word that has the same or almost the same meaning as another word. For example, **cool** and **chilly** are synonyms. Read each clue. Then write the Spelling or Review Word that is a synonym.

1. garbage
2. wind
3. pal
4. scare
5. a show
6. unafraid

> **Spell Chat**
> Challenge the person next to you to think of two other compound words with a consonant blend with r.

Ⓑ Word Study: **Compound Words**

A compound word is made up of two or more words, as in **blackbird**. Write the spelling word that can be joined with each word below to make a compound word.

ground	print	trap	brain
drive	grand	drift	cross

7. _____ door
8. _____ parent
9. _____ walk
10. _____ out
11. _____ hog
12. _____ storm
13. _____ way
14. _____ wood

Ⓒ Write

Write a sentence about the beach or the sea. Use these spelling words.

front   crab

_____

_____

Spelling Words

breeze	front
brain	grand
crab	ground
cross	print
drift	program
drive	trap
frighten	trash
friend	

Review	Challenge
splash	tremendous
spoil	grouchy
brave	

My Words

_____

_____

_____

Spelling Words

breeze	front
brain	grand
crab	ground
cross	print
drift	program
drive	trap
frighten	trash
friend LOOKOUT WORD	

Review	Challenge
splash	tremendous
spoil	grouchy
brave	

My Words

Quick Write

Write a question about something you would like to know. Use a spelling word.

You may wish to do this activity on a computer.

A Write Interview Questions

Imagine that you are going to interview a park ranger visiting your class. Think of three questions to ask the ranger about the parks or beaches in your area. Use spelling words and other words that have consonant blends with **r**.

Tip
Are you writing a question? Be sure to use a question mark at the end.

B Proofread

Rick wrote these three interview questions. He made two spelling errors, one punctuation error, and forgot a capital letter. Correct the errors.

1. Do any parks have a summer program for kids

2. We don't want to spoyl the parks. how can visitors keep trash from piling up?

3. Are people allowed to driv on state beaches?

PROOFREADING MARKS

∧ Add
⊙ Add a period
ℓ Take out
⟲∧ Move
≡ Capital letter
/ Small letter
¶ Indent paragraph

Now proofread your questions. Check for spelling, punctuation, and capitalization.

A Use the Dictionary: **Verb Endings**

What do you find at the end of a dictionary entry? If the word is a verb, you will probably find the word with its **-ing** and **-ed** endings. Read these sample entries.

> **blame** /blām/ *verb*
> To say that something is someone's fault.
> ▶ **blaming, blamed**
> **cross** /kros/ *verb*
> To go from one side to the other.
> ▶ **crossing, crossed**

Finish these sentences with the correct form of **blame** or **cross**.

The children are _____ the street.

No one _____ them for not wanting to stop.

Now write your own sentence, using **drive + -ing.**

_____

_____

B Test Yourself

Change the underlined part of each word to make a spelling word.

1. <u>c</u>ash	**5.** <u>sn</u>ap	**9.** <u>f</u>ound	**13.** <u>h</u>ive
2. <u>m</u>int	**6.** <u>t</u>ab	**10.** <u>br</u>ighten	**14.** <u>st</u>and
3. <u>f</u>ont	**7.** <u>sn</u>eeze	**11.** <u>l</u>ift	**15.** <u>t</u>angram
4. <u>f</u>iend	**8.** <u>t</u>rain	**12.** <u>b</u>oss	

For Tomorrow...
Get ready to share the words you discovered that begin with a consonant blend with r. Remember to study for your test!

Get Word Wise
The word **trash** comes from an Old Norwegian word, **tros**. It meant "fallen leaves and twigs." In the fall, trees get rid of their leaves. Today, something you get rid of is also called **trash**.

Word Study Strategy

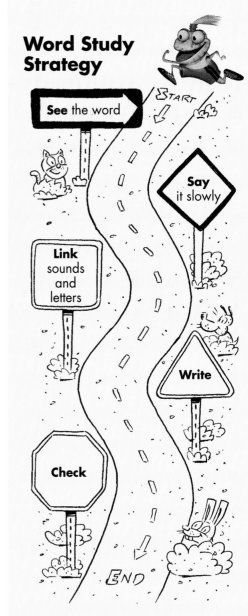

START

See the word

Say it slowly

Link sounds and letters

Write

Check

END

Consonant Blends With s

A See and Say

Spelling Words

scout	smooth
scream	snack
scrub	spell
skunk	spend
skin	straight **LOOKOUT WORD**
slip	sweet
sled	swamp
smell	

Review	Challenge
friend	scribble
first	snowflakes
stamp	

My Words

_____

_____

_____

_____

The Spelling Concept

scout	skunk	scrub
straight	spell	sweet
slip	snack	smell

The letter **s** joins with many other consonants to form consonant blends.

B Link Sounds and Letters

Say each word. Listen for the consonant blend with **s**. Sort the spelling words by their consonant blends.

"Ice cream!" I scream.

MEMORY JOGGER

Word Sort

sc	scr	sk
sl	sm	sn
sp	str	sw

C Write and Check

Use spelling words to write your own tongue twister.

_____

_____

TONGUE TWISTER

See six smooth, skinny snakes skip, slip, slither, and slide.

Say it fast!

A Build Vocabulary: **Related Words**

Read the words and think about how they go together.
Then write the spelling word that goes with each set.

1. nose, scent, _____
2. write, proofread, _____
3. money, buy, _____
4. yell, shout, _____
5. wash, clean, _____
6. snow, hill, _____
7. munch, nibble, _____
8. alligator, soggy, _____
9. fur, fleece, _____
10. slide, fall, _____

Spell Chat

Turn to a classmate.
Say two words related to
a Spelling or Review Word.
See if he or she can say
the spelling word that
goes with them.

B Word Study: **Opposites**

Write the Spelling or Review
Word that means the opposite
of each word below.

11. sour   14. enemy

12. rough   15. last

13. crooked

C Write

Write a sentence, using these words.

scout   skunk

_____

_____

Spelling Words

scout	smooth
scream	snack
scrub	spell
skunk	spend
skin	straight
slip	sweet
sled	swamp
smell	

Review	Challenge
friend	scribble
first	snowflakes
stamp	

My Words

_____

_____

_____

_____

Spelling Words

scout
scream
scrub
skunk
skin
slip
sled
smell

smooth
snack
spell
spend
straight LOOKOUT WORD
sweet
swamp

Review	Challenge
friend	scribble
first	snowflakes
stamp	

My Words

_____

_____

_____

_____

Quick Write
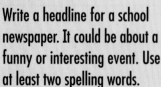
Write a headline for a school newspaper. It could be about a funny or interesting event. Use at least two spelling words.

A Write an Article

You may wish to do this activity on a computer.

Write an article for your local newspaper about something special that happened to you or someone you know. Use four spelling words.

B Proofread

Kim wrote this article. She made three spelling errors. She also forgot one comma and a capital letter. Correct the errors.

Tip
Use commas between words in a series to help make the meaning clear.

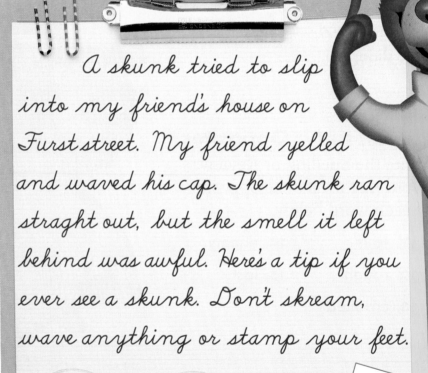

A skunk tried to slip into my friend's house on Furst street. My friend yelled and waved his cap. The skunk ran straght out, but the smell it left behind was awful. Here's a tip if you ever see a skunk. Don't skream, wave anything or stamp your feet.

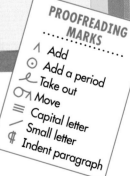

Proofread your article. Check your spelling, and be sure you put capital letters and commas where they are needed.

PROOFREADING MARKS

∧ Add
⊙ Add a period
ℓ Take out
↰ Move
≡ Capital letter
╱ Small letter
¶ Indent paragraph

A Use the Dictionary: Synonyms

Synonyms are words with similar meanings. Dictionaries give synonyms for some words. Look at these synonyms for **slide.**

> **Synonyms: slide**
> *Slide* means to move easily over a smooth surface.
> *Slip* means to slide accidentally and lose your balance.
> *Glide* means to move smoothly, easily, and usually silently.
> *Skid* means to slide sideways and out of control.

Write the best synonym to complete each sentence.

Someone might _____ and fall on an icy sidewalk.

Skaters _____ quietly across the ice.

A patch of ice on the road can cause a car to _____ .

Children love to _____ down the hill on their sleds.

B Test Yourself

Write the spelling words that begin with the same consonant blends as these words.

1. street
2–3. sky
4. snake
5–6. smile
7–8. spot
9–10. slide
11. scare
12–13. scrap
14–15. swing

For Tomorrow...
Get ready to share the words you discovered that have consonant blends with s. Remember to study for your test!

Get Word Wise

Skunk is a very American word. English settlers learned it from Native Americans. The English had never seen a skunk before and didn't have a name for it. The names of many animals come from Native American languages. **Raccoon**, **moose**, and **chipmunk** are a few.

Word Study Strategy

See the word
START
Say it slowly
Link sounds and letters
Write
Check
END

Spelling Words

thick	gather
thunder	together
throat	rather
truth	other
bath	mother
bother (LOOKOUT WORD)	another
father	nothing
feather	

Review	Challenge
straight	author
porch	theater
these	

My Words

Words With Digraph th

A See and Say

The Spelling Concept

th	**th**under
th	fa**th**er

Two letters can stand for one sound. The letters **th** stand for the sound at the beginning of **thunder.** They also stand for the sound in the middle of **father.**

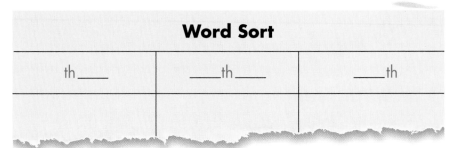

U always tell the truth.

MEMORY JOGGER

B Link Sounds and Letters

Say each spelling word. Listen for the sound **th** makes. Look for where **th** appears in each word. Then sort the spelling words on a chart like this one.

Word Sort		
th_____	_____th_____	_____th

C Write and Check

Which words in the joke have **th**? Write them.

_____

_____

JOKE
Why does your brother always take a cold bath?

He doesn't want to get in hot water!

A Build Vocabulary: **Opposites**

Some words, such as **push** and **pull,** are opposites. Write the Spelling or Review Word that means the opposite of each word.

1. a lie
2. thin
3. crooked
4. apart
5. everything
6. mother

Spell Chat
Ask a classmate to name an opposite with th for the words **south, rough,** and **sister.**

B Word Study: **Letter Patterns**

The underlined word in each sentence does not make sense. Fix it. Replace one or two letters with **th.** Then write the spelling word.

7. I'm sorry to <u>bolder</u> you.
8. I hope my <u>mover</u> brought an umbrella to work.
9. The storm began with a crash of <u>blunder</u>.
10. If it rains very hard, maybe we won't need a <u>band</u>!
11. I would <u>racer</u> walk than take the bus.
12. Please help me <u>gander</u> the toys in the yard.
13. You take this toy, and I'll take the <u>offer</u>.
14. This blue and green <u>feaster</u> came from a peacock.

C Write

Write a short message that you might send a friend. Use these spelling words: **throat, another.**

_____

_____

Be a Spelling Sleuth
Look in the yellow pages of the telephone book. Find names of products and stores with the letters th such as **clothing.** Keep a list.

Spelling Words

thick	gather
thunder	together
throat	rather
truth	other
bath	mother
bother	another
father	nothing
feather	

LOOKOUT WORD

Review	Challenge
straight	author
porch	theater
these	

My Words

_____

_____

_____

_____

Spelling Words

thick	gather
thunder	together
throat	rather
truth	other
bath	mother
bother	another
father	nothing
feather	

 LOOKOUT WORD

Review	Challenge
straight	author
porch	theater
these	

My Words

_____

_____

_____

_____

Quick Write

Use three spelling words with **th** to write a sentence that exaggerates something.

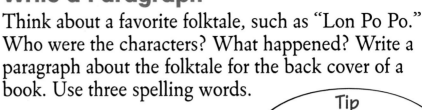

You may wish to do this activity on a computer.

Ⓐ Write a Paragraph

Think about a favorite folktale, such as "Lon Po Po." Who were the characters? What happened? Write a paragraph about the folktale for the back cover of a book. Use three spelling words.

Tip

When you write, check your sentences to see that they have a subject and a predicate.

Ⓑ Proofread

Carlos wrote about Johnny Appleseed. He made three spelling errors and one punctuation error. One sentence is missing a subject. Correct the errors.

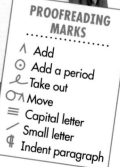

> Everyone eats apples theze days. We can thank Johnny Appleseed for that! Long ago, he decided to gater apple seeds. Then walked hundreds of miles to plant them. Soon the country was thik with apple trees Discover why Johnny became the apple of everyone's eye.

PROOFREADING MARKS

∧ Add
⊙ Add a period
ℓ Take out
↻↱ Move
≡ Capital letter
／ Small letter
¶ Indent paragraph

Now proofread your paragraph. Check for spelling and punctuation. Be sure every sentence has a subject and a predicate.

A Use the Dictionary: **Multiple Meanings**

A dictionary entry numbers each meaning for a word.
Read the entry for **thunder**.

> **thun·der** (thun dər)
>   1. *noun* The loud, rumbling sound that comes after a
>   flash of lightning. Thunder is caused by the expansion
>   of air that has been heated by lightning.
>   2. *verb* To make loud noise like thunder.
>   *The trucks thundered past.*

Write the number of the meaning of **thunder** that fits
the sentence.

_____ A herd of buffalo thundered across the plains.

Write a sentence for **thunder** using the other meaning.

_____

B Test Yourself

In a word math problem, you subtract and add letters.
For example, **pond - nd + rch = porch**. Complete
each problem and write the spelling words.

1. none - ne + thing =
2. bird - ird + ath =
3. tool - ol + gether =
4. trip - ip + uth =
5. gasp - sp + ther =
6. farm - rm + ther =
7. ring - ing + ather =
8. brother - br =

9. thin - in + ick =
10. threw - ew + oat =
11. and - d + other =
12. month - nth + ther =
13. thumb - umb + under =
14. bat - at + other =
15. fear - r + ther =

For Tomorrow...
Get ready to share the th words
you discovered, and remember to
study for your test!

Get Word Wise

In Norse mythology, there was a god
named Thor. He rode across the sky
in a giant chariot. The word **thunder**
comes from the loud rumbling sound
of Thor's chariot. The next time you
hear thunder, think of
Thor racing across
the sky!

Word Study Strategy

See the word

START

Say it slowly

Link sounds and letters

Write

Check

END

March

Months of the Year

Spelling Words

January	September
February	October
March	November
April	December
May	month
June	monthly
July	year
August	

LOOKOUT WORD

Review	Challenge
bother	calendar
noon	annual
weekend	

My Words

A See and Say

The Spelling Concept

November	January
December	February

The months of the year are easier to spell when you look for familiar patterns.

R U ready for February?

MEMORY JOGGER

B Link Sounds and Letters

Say each spelling word. Listen for patterns that are the same. Then fill in the chart to sort the spelling words.

Word Sort

one-syllable words	two-syllable words	words that end with ber	words that end with uary

C Write and Check

Write the two spelling words in the well-known poem that have the same ending.

_____

_____

THE MONTHS

Thirty days hath September, April, June, and November.
All the rest have thirty-one,
Excepting February alone,
And that has twenty-eight days clear,
And twenty-nine in each leap year.

A Build Vocabulary: Sequence of Months

Think about the order in which the months happen each year. Use each clue below to write the name of a month.

1. the month after March and before May

2. the next to last month of the year

3. the first month of the year

4. the month before June

5. the last month of the year

6. the month between June and August

7. the month after January

Spell Chat
Challenge a friend to say the names of the months in backward order from December to January.

B Word Study: Proper Nouns

A proper noun names a particular person, place, or thing. **July** is a proper noun. Every proper noun begins with a capital letter.

Complete each sentence with the spelling word that begins with the same letter as most of the other words in the sentence.

June   August   March   September   October

8. Maria makes mango marmalade in _____.

9. Oscar only orders oranges in _____.

10. Susanna surfs and swims in _____.

11. Jerry jumps for joy in _____.

12. Aunt Agatha always goes abroad in _____.

C Write

Write two sentences using **month, monthly,** and **year.**

_____

_____

Be a Spelling Sleuth

Check places where you might see a calendar, for example, in a bank or supermarket. Look for the names of months. Keep a list. Which month did you see most often?

Spelling Words

January	September
February	October
March	November
April	December
May	month
June	monthly
July	year
August	

LOOKOUT WORD

Review	Challenge
bother	calendar
noon	annual
weekend	

My Words

_____

_____

_____

_____

_____

Spelling Words

January	September
February	October
March	November
April	December
May	month
June	monthly
July	year
August	

(March: LOOKOUT WORD)

Review	Challenge
bother	calendar
noon	annual
weekend	

My Words

Quick Write
Make a list of the birthdays of
your friends and family members.

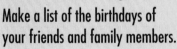

Write and Proofread

You may wish to do this activity on a computer.

A. Write a Nonfiction Narrative

Write about the month of the year that you like best. If you can't choose just one, write about as many as you like. Tell why the month is special for you. Use as many spelling words as you can.

> **Tip**
> Be sure that every sentence has a subject that tells who or what the sentence is about.

B. Proofread

Jamie wrote about her two favorite months. Her writing contains three spelling errors and one capitalization error. One sentence is missing the subject. Correct her errors.

> I like may because it's in the spring. Can play soccer and baseball with my friends on the weakend. I also like Oktober. My dad and I have our birthdays in that munth. I also like to see the leaves change colors.

PROOFREADING MARKS

∧ Add
⊙ Add a period
ℓ Take out
↶ Move
≡ Capital letter
/ Small letter
¶ Indent paragraph

Now proofread your paragraph.
Check your spelling and capitalization.
Be sure each sentence has a subject.

Ⓐ Use the Dictionary: Syllables

A dictionary shows you how to pronounce a word and how many syllables the word has. Look at this dictionary entry for **February**. It has four syllables, and there are two ways to pronounce it.

Feb·ru·ar·y /feb rōō er ē or **feb** yōō er ē/
noun The second month of the year. February has 28 days except in a leap year, when it has 29 days.

Read the names of the months and their pronunciations. Notice how many syllables each month has.

Jan·u·ar·y /jan yōō er ē/   **Sep·tem·ber /**sep **tem** bər/
A·pril /ā prəl/   **Oc·to·ber /**ok **tō** bər/
May /mā/   **No·vem·ber /**nō **vem** bər/
Ju·ly /jōō **lī**/   **De·cem·ber /**di **sem** bər/

Write the names of the months that have three syllables.

_____   _____

_____   _____

Ⓑ Test Yourself

Write a spelling word for each clue.

1. 365 days
2. after December
3. the eighth month
4. one of twelve
5. Thanksgiving Day
6. rhymes with **day**
7. before April
8. once a month

9. begins with **O**
10. between March and May
11. shortest month
12. rhymes with **moon**
13. Labor Day
14. Independence Day
15. end of the year

For Tomorrow...
Get ready to share the names of the months you saw, and remember to study for your test!

Get Word Wise

July and **August** were named for Roman emperors—Julius Caesar and Augustus Caesar. Augustus was unhappy because his month originally had only 30 days while Julius's had 31. So calendar-makers took a day from February to make both months 31 days long!

Word Study Strategy

START
See the word
Say it slowly
Link sounds and letters
Write
Check
END

Amber's Adventure

Complete each sentence with a spelling word.

another September nothing plain spend

It was early in (1) . School had not started yet. Amber sat in her aunt and uncle's backyard. There were no kids to play with and (2) much to do. She'd just finished one book and wasn't ready to start (3) one. She was thinking, "How will I (4) the day?" Then she saw something odd. It was there in (5) sight!

flash ground smell straight swamp

Amber walked (6) to the gate. In a (7) , she opened it and stepped out of the yard into a place she had never seen before. She sniffed the air. It had a wet (8) . "How strange," she thought. The (9) felt squishy under her feet. Amber had stepped into a (10) !

plan slide snack splash truth

Amber heard a (11) . She looked and saw a snake (12) into the water. Maybe leaving the yard wasn't such a good (13) . As she turned, she came face to face with an alligator. She did not want to be the alligator's (14) , so she raced through the gate and back to the house.

"Where have you been?" asked her aunt. "How did your feet get so wet?"

Amber told the (15) , of course. "I went out to see the swamp," she said.

"What swamp?" asked her aunt. "We're in the middle of the city. There are no swamps in the city!"

Word Associations

bother   gloves   thunder
friend   glass

Write the spelling word that belongs in each group.

1. cup, plate, _____

2. hands, mittens, _____

3. pal, buddy, _____

4. rain, lightning, _____

5. annoy, pester, _____

In Other Words...

front   spell   March
brain   cross

Write the spelling word that fits the meaning of each sentence.

6. The third month of the year is _____.

7. If you write something correctly, you know how to

_____.

8. Someone who is frowning is probably

_____.

9. If you are first in line, you are in _____.

10. When you think, you use your _____.

Letter Mix-Up

Mix up the letters in each word to make a new word. There is a clue in ( ).
Hint: Use a consonant blend in each new word.

owls _____ (not fast)

diver _____ (go in a car)

creams _____ (shout)

idles _____ (slip)

yam _____ (a month)

My Words

month	grand
splash	slow
plant	slip
thunder	year
flash	father
program	together
ground	September
another	

Tip
Don't leave out any of the letters in a consonant blend.

PROOFREADING MARKS
....
∧ Add
⊙ Add a period
ℓ Take out
⌒ Move
= Capital letter
/ Small letter
¶ Indent paragraph

News Flash!

A newspaper headline tells what a news story is about. Read each headline. Then write the first sentence of the news story. Use two or more spelling words in each sentence.

1. Another Win for Team

_____

2. Father of Six Wins in Garden Show

_____

3. Storm Strikes Boston

_____

4. Big Mess Follows Storm

_____

5. School Program a Hit

_____

Look back at My Words and the words you misspelled in your Unit 5 Posttests. Use them to start another article.

6. Third Grader Amazes Everyone!

_____

Read About It

Choose one of the headlines you wrote about. Finish the news story you started. Then proofread your article for spelling, capitalization, and punctuation.

_____

_____

What Month Is It?

Read each sentence from a student's journal. Write the name of the month it was written in.

July February November January
December October March June

Spelling Matters!

1. This is a new year, and I'm going to write in my journal every day. _____

2. We had a picnic in the park on Independence Day. _____

3. This is the first day of spring! _____

4. Tomorrow is the first of November, and it's my mom's birthday. _____

5. It snowed again on President's Day. _____

6. I love the smell of turkey and pumpkin pie. _____

7. The first day of summer and Father's Day are on the same day this year. _____

8. Next week, our class is presenting a holiday play for the end of the year. _____

Spelling Words

afternoon	homework
airport	popcorn
almost LOOKOUT WORD	railroad
backyard	sidewalk
barefoot	sunshine
birthday	tiptoe
downstairs	upstairs
grasshopper	

Review	Challenge
February	breakfast
airplane	cupboard
sometimes	

My Words

_____

_____

_____

_____

Compound Words

A See and Say

The Spelling Concept

side + walk = sidewalk
after + noon = afternoon
pop + corn = popcorn

A compound word is made up of two words joined together. For example, the compound word **popcorn** is made up of the words **pop** and **corn.**

> Almost — It's **not all** there!

MEMORY JOGGER

B Link Sounds and Letters

Say each spelling word. Then say the two smaller words that make up the compound word. Sort the words on a diagram like this. Write the compound words in the middle.

Word Sort

small word   small word

compound word

C Write and Check

Read the joke. What are the compound words? Write them.

_____

_____

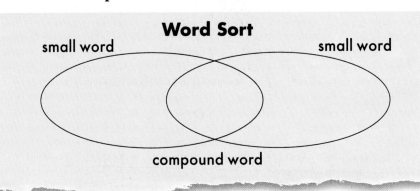

JOKE

What is green, lives in your backyard, and can jump a mile a minute?

a grasshopper with hiccups

A Build Vocabulary: **Word Meaning**

Write a compound word for each meaning by combining a word from column A with a word from column B. Look out for a spelling change in one of the words.

A	B
bare	hopper
side	noon
all	walk
rail	foot
grass	road
after	most

1. train tracks
2. hopping insect
3. walkway
4. without shoes and socks
5. very nearly
6. time between morning and evening

B Word Study: **Build Compound Words**

One word in each compound word is underlined. Write the spelling word with the same word.

7. <u>toe</u>nail
8. <u>sun</u>burn
9. <u>back</u>pack
10. <u>down</u>town
11. <u>up</u>hill
12. <u>home</u>made
13. <u>air</u>line
14. <u>birth</u>place
15. <u>corn</u>stalk

C Write

Write a sign for a sidewalk sale. Use three spelling words.

_____

Spell Chat
Challenge the person next to you to think of two other compound words.

Be a Spelling Sleuth
Read labels on food packages for more compound words such as **buttermilk**, **chickpeas**, and **tunafish**. Keep a list of words you see.

Spelling Words

afternoon	homework
airport	popcorn
almost	railroad
backyard	sidewalk
barefoot	sunshine
birthday	tiptoe
downstairs	upstairs
grasshopper	

Review	Challenge
February	breakfast
airplane	cupboard
sometimes	

My Words

_____
_____
_____

Spelling Words

afternoon	homework
airport	popcorn
almost (LOOKOUT WORD)	railroad
backyard	sidewalk
barefoot	sunshine
birthday	tiptoe
downstairs	upstairs
grasshopper	

Review	Challenge
February	breakfast
airplane	cupboard
sometimes	

My Words

Quick Write

Write a two-line verse. It can be silly or serious. Include a compound word in each line.

You may wish to do this activity on a computer.

A Write a Poem

Write a poem about a party you had or would like to have. First, brainstorm a list of spelling words and other compound words you might use in your poem. Then, start to write.

B Proofread

Alicia wrote this poem. She made three spelling errors and one capitalization error. In one sentence, she used the wrong homophone. Correct the errors.

Tip
If you use any words that are homophones, be sure you write the right one.

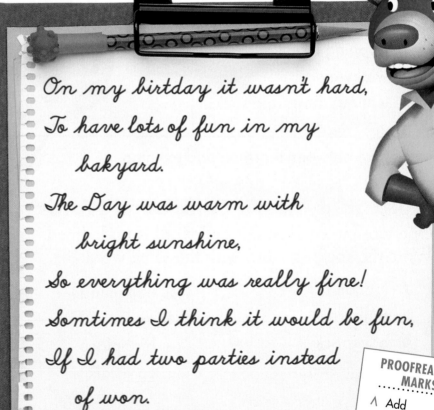

On my birtday it wasn't hard,
To have lots of fun in my
    bakyard.
The Day was warm with
    bright sunshine,
So everything was really fine!
Somtimes I think it would be fun,
If I had two parties instead
    of won.

PROOFREADING MARKS

∧ Add
⊙ Add a period
ℓ Take out
↶↷ Move
≡ Capital letter
/ Small letter
¶ Indent paragraph

Now proofread the poem you wrote. Check your spelling, punctuation, and capitalization.

A Use the Dictionary: **Word Histories**

Some dictionaries give the histories of words. They tell you what language the word first came from, how it was spelled, and what it meant.

Word History

Popcorn was one of the earliest corn crops that Native Americans grew. They used it for decoration, as food, and in special ceremonies. The word popcorn was first used in the early 1800s. It probably was named for the "popping" sound that you hear when making the delicious snack.

Read the word histories. Write the spelling word that fits each entry.

_____ *noun* Work assigned at school that is to be done at home. [from Old English *ham,* home, and Old English *weorc,* work.]

_____ *noun* a track of double rails for a train. [From Latin *regula,* straight piece of wood, and Old English *rad,* road.]

B Test Yourself

Each of the words below is made up of three words instead of two. Leave out one of the words to make a spelling word.

1. uphillstairs
2. tiptoenail
3. insidewalk
4. sunburnshine
5. popcornfield
6. grasslandhopper
7. barefootball
8. backyardstick
9. birthdaytime
10. afternoontime
11. airplaneport
12. alwaysmost
13. downtownstairs
14. homeschoolwork
15. railwayroad

Word Study Strategy

See the word · START · Say it slowly · Link sounds and letters · Write · Check · END

For Tomorrow...
Get ready to share the compound words you discovered, and remember to study for your test!

Spelling Words

can't	I'll
didn't	we'll
don't	I'm
won't *LOOKOUT WORD*	you're
here's	they're
there's	I've
it's	you've
what's	

Review	Challenge
almost	shouldn't
plant	should've
whose	

My Words

_____

_____

_____

Contractions

Ⓐ See and Say

The Spelling Concept

did + not = didn't
we + will = we'll
you + have = you've
they + are = they're

A contraction is a word made by putting two words together and leaving out letters. An apostrophe takes the place of letters that are left out.

No, I will not! No, I won't!

MEMORY JOGGER

Ⓑ Link Sounds and Letters

Say each spelling word. Think about the words that go together to form the contraction. Then sort the words on a chart like this one.

Word Sort

not	is	am/are	will	have

Ⓒ Write and Check

Write the contractions in the riddle.

_____

_____

RIDDLE
Why won't the pony sing?

(because it's a little hoarse (horse))

A Build Vocabulary: **Contractions**

Write the spelling word that is the contraction of the underlined words. Remember the apostrophe.

1. <u>We will</u> go to the ball game tomorrow.
2. <u>I have</u> an extra ticket.
3. Maybe <u>it is</u> possible for Ann to come.
4. <u>Here is</u> her phone number.
5. Can you call her if <u>you have</u> a chance?
6. <u>There is</u> someone ringing the doorbell.
7. <u>What is</u> the time right now?
8. <u>I am</u> waiting for my friends to visit.
9. I think <u>they are</u> here.
10. I hope <u>you are</u> going to stay.

B Word Study: **Opposites**

Some words, such as **are** and **aren't**, are opposites. Make the sentences below mean the opposite of what they say. Write the contraction that is the opposite of the underlined word.

11. Some children really <u>do</u> like spinach.
12. You <u>can</u> expect them to eat a lot of it.
13. They <u>will</u> call it their favorite food.
14. The children at our school certainly <u>did</u>.

C Write

Write a sentence to persuade someone to try a new food. Use **I'll** and another spelling word.

_____

_____

Spell Chat
Challenge the person next to you to use three contractions in a sentence or a question.

Be a Spelling Sleuth
Look at the dialogue in stories for more contractions. Keep a list of the contractions you find and where you found them.

Spelling Words

can't	I'll
didn't	we'll
don't	I'm
won't	you're
here's	they're
there's	I've
it's	you've
what's	

Review	Challenge
almost	shouldn't
plant	should've
whose	

My Words

_____

_____

_____

_____

Spelling Words

can't   I'll
didn't   we'll
don't   I'm
won't   you're
here's   they're
there's   I've
it's   you've
what's

Review	Challenge
almost	shouldn't
plant	should've
whose	

My Words

Quick Write

Write an announcement for a school event. Use at least two contractions.

You may wish to do this activity on a computer.

A Write a Note

Write a note inviting a friend to join you in an afterschool program. Give reasons why you think your friend would enjoy it. Use as least two spelling words.

B Proofread

Eileen wrote this note. She made three spelling errors and one punctuation error. In one contraction, she put the apostrophe in the wrong place. Correct the errors.

Tip
Remember to use apostrophes to show where the letters are left out in contractions.

Dear Sarina,

I've joined the soccer team, and you should, too. Your good at sports. You'll be great at soccer. Besides, its fun!

It's September and allmost time for the season to start. Why do'nt you come along next week

Eileen

PROOFREADING MARKS

∧ Add
⊙ Add a period
ℓ Take out
↷ Move
≡ Capital letter
／ Small letter
¶ Indent paragraph

Now proofread your note. Check spelling, capitalization, and correct punctuation, especially in contractions.

Ⓐ Use the Dictionary: **Homophones**

The dictionary gives you the meanings of words.
It will also tell you if a word has homophones.
A homophone is a word that sounds like another word
but has a different spelling and meaning. Read the
dictionary entry for **they're**.

they're /ᵺâr/ *contraction*
A short form of *they are*. **They're** sounds like
there and **their**.

Write a sentence for each of the homophones: **they're**,
there, and **their**.

_____

_____

_____

Ⓑ Test Yourself

Figure out which letter or letters are missing from each
contraction. Then write the contraction.

1. d _ dn't
2. d _ n't
3. w _ 'll
4. y _ _ 're
5. y _ _ 've

6. _ 'm
7. _ 've
8. _ 'll
9. th _ re's
10. th _ y're

11. h _ re's
12. wh _ t's
13. _ t's
14. c _ n't
15. w _ n't

For Tomorrow...
Get ready to share the
contractions you discovered,
and remember to study
for your test!

Contractions are good examples of
how written words can come from
speech. When people speak, they
often run words together. Many
contractions are made by combining
helping verbs and the word **not**.
For example, it's quicker to
say **aren't** than
are not.

**Word Study
Strategy**

START

See the word

Say it slowly

Link sounds and letters

Write

Check

END

Spelling Words

begin	swimming
began	step
beginning	stepped
grin	stepping
grinned	trip
grinning	tripped
swim	tripping
swam	LOOKOUT WORD

Review	Challenge
won't	baby-sitting
drive	window-shopping
done	

My Words

_____

_____

_____

_____

Words That End With -ed and -ing

A See and Say

The Spelling Concept

$$grin + \underline{n} + ed = gri\underline{nn}ed$$

$$step + \underline{p} + ing = ste\underline{pp}ing$$

When a verb ends with one consonant letter that follows a short vowel sound, you must double the final consonant before adding **-ed** or **-ing.**

*Take an extra step. Double the **p** to get ste**pp**ed.*

MEMORY JOGGER

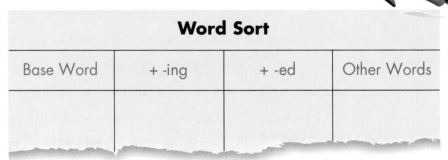

B Link Sounds and Letters

Say each spelling word. Listen for the base word. Listen for the endings **-ed** and **-ing**. Sort the words on a chart like this one.

Word Sort			
Base Word	+ -ing	+ -ed	Other Words

C Write and Check

Write the spelling words in the elephant joke.

_____

_____

ELEPHANT JOKE

Why did the grinning elephant jump into the swimming pool?

He wanted to make a big splash!

A Build Vocabulary: **Synonyms**

Synonyms are words with the same or almost the same meaning. Write the spelling word that is a synonym for each of these words.

1. smile
2. stumble
3. walk
4. start
5. paddle, float
6. started

Spell Chat
Challenge a classmate to write synonyms for three spelling words that end in -ed or -ing.

B Word Study: **Verb Endings**

Add **-ed** or **-ing** to the spelling word so that it completes each sentence correctly. Write the word.

7. swim — The dog was _____ in the lake.
8. trip — The hiker _____ over a tree root.
9. begin — The baby is _____ to walk.
10. step — The batter _____ up to the plate.
11. grin — The winner was _____ from ear to ear.
12. trip — People are _____ on the torn carpet.
13. step — You're _____ on my foot!
14. grin — Everyone _____ when you told the story.

C Write

Write a message to a friend. Use these Spelling Words and Review Words.

done   swam   drive

_____

_____

_____

Be a Spelling Sleuth

Look in chapter books for verbs that end with -ed and -ing such as **slipping** and **hopped.** Make a list of the words you find.

Spelling Words

begin	swimming
began	step
beginning	stepped
grin	stepping
grinned	trip
grinning	tripped
swim	tripping
swam	

Review	Challenge
won't	baby - sitting
drive	window-shopping
done	

My Words

_____

_____

_____

Spelling Words

begin	swimming
began	step
beginning	stepped
grin	stepping
grinned	trip
grinning	tripped
swim	tripping
swam	*LOOKOUT WORD*

Review	Challenge
won't	baby-sitting
drive	window-shopping
done	

My Words

Quick Write 🖊️

Write a list of things you want to do this summer. Use two spelling words.

Ⓐ Write a List of Tips

You may wish to do this activity on a computer.

What sport do you like? What would you tell someone who wanted to learn it? Write some tips. Include at least three spelling words in your tips.

Ⓑ Proofread

Rashid wrote some tips about swimming. He made four spelling errors, one punctuation error, and one error in capitalization. Correct them.

Tip
Remember to capitalize names of particular people, places, and things.

Swimming Tips
- *A good place to swim is Rainbow Pool in Sunset park.*
- *When you're begining, swim a little every day.*
- *Wear goggles so water won't get in your eyes*
- *Be careful when you stip out of the pool.*
- *Soon you'll be swiming like a fish!*

PROOFREADING MARKS
- ∧ Add
- ⊙ Add a period
- ℓ Take out
- ⟲ Move
- ≡ Capital letter
- / Small letter
- ¶ Indent paragraph

Now proofread your tips. Check your spelling, punctuation, and capitalization of proper nouns.

Ⓐ Use a Dictionary: **Pronunciations**

A dictionary shows you how to say a word. After each entry word, there is a pronunciation that uses letters and symbols to show how to say the word. Look at these words and their pronunciations.

> **swam** /swam/
> **grin·ning** /grin ing/
> **drive** /drīv/
> **swim·ming** /swim ing/

Write the spelling for the words in / /. Use the pronunciation key in your Spelling Dictionary. It will help you read the pronunciations.

/trip/ _____   /swim/ _____

/wōnt/_____   /step ing/ _____

Ⓑ Test Yourself

Figure out the missing letter or letters in each word. Write the spelling word.

1. t_ip
2. swi_ _ing
3. ste_ _ed
4. b_gin
5. gri_ _ing

6. s_am
7. tri_ _ing
8. g_in
9. b_gan
10. gri_ _ed

11. s_im
12. begi_ _ing
13. s_ep
14. tri_ _ed
15. ste_ _ing

For Tomorrow...
Get ready to share the verbs with -ed and -ing you have discovered, and remember to study for the test!

Word Study Strategy

START

See the word

Say it slowly

Link sounds and letters

Write

Check

END

Learn and Spell

Final e With -ed and -ing

Ⓐ See and Say

Spelling Words

dance	moving
danced	use
dancing	used
hope	using
hoped	waste
hoping	wasted
move	wasting
moved	

LOOKOUT WORD

Review	Challenge
swam	scrambled
spend	giggling
skate	

My Words

_____

_____

_____

_____

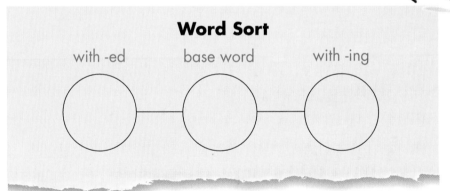

The Spelling Concept

hope + ed = hoped
dance + ing = dancing

Some verbs end with a consonant and the letter **e**.
To add **-ed** or **-ing,** drop the **e.**

Drop the **e.**
Then add **-ed.**
Do the same
for **-ing**!

MEMORY
JOGGER

Ⓑ Link Sounds and Letters

Say each spelling word. Listen for the base
word. Then listen for the ending **-ed** or **-ing.**
Write the words in a web like the one below.

Word Sort

with -ed   base word   with -ing

◯————————◯————————◯

Ⓒ Write and Check

Write the spelling words in the
daffynition. Then use another
form of those verbs in a
sentence.

DAFFYNITION
What's a snowball?

a place where
snowflakes are
hoping to dance

_____

_____

_____

A Build Vocabulary: **Related Words**

Write the spelling word that best fits
in each group.

1. wish, want, _____
2. step, sway, _____
3. push, carry, _____
4. spoil, be careless, _____

Spell Chat

Challenge a classmate to
think of two verbs that end
in a consonant and **e**.
Then ask him or her to
spell the words with the
endings -ed and -ing.

B Word Study: **Verb Forms**

Verbs that end with **-ed** tell about
something that has already happened. Verbs
that end with **-ing** are used with helping
verbs such as **am**, **is**, **are**, **was**, and **were**.
Complete the phrases in each column
with the correct form of the verb in ( ).

Yesterday we…	Today we are…
5. (move) ___ the boxes,	10. (move) ___ our feet,
6. (use) ___ our heads,	11. (use) ___ our imaginations,
7. (hope) ___ for rain,	12. (hope) ___ to win,
8. (waste) ___ time, and	13. (waste) ___ no time, and
9. (dance) ___ a jig.	14. (dance) ___ in the rain.

C Write

Write an ad for recycling. Use these Spelling and
Review Words.

waste   use   spend

_____

_____

_____

Be a Spelling Sleuth

Look in comic books and comic strips
for verbs that end with
-ed and -ing. Write the
words you find.

Spelling Words

dance	moving
danced	use
dancing	used
hope	using
hoped	waste
hoping	wasted
move	wasting
moved	

Review	Challenge
swam	scrambled
spend	giggling
skate	

My Words

_____

_____

_____

_____

Spelling Words

dance	moving
danced	use
dancing	used
hope	using
hoped	waste 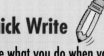 LOOKOUT WORD
hoping	wasted
move	wasting
moved	

Review	Challenge
swam	scrambled
spend	giggling
skate	

My Words

_____

_____

_____

Quick Write 🖉

Write what you do when you hear your favorite kind of music. Use as many spelling words as you can.

You may wish to do this activity on a computer.

A Write a Biographical Sketch

A friend of yours has just finished recording a CD. Write a biographical sketch for the cover. Think of some interesting facts about your friend's life.

Tip

Make sure your subjects and verbs agree in person and number.

B Proofread

Sasha wrote this biographical sketch. She made three spelling errors and one punctuation error. In one sentence, she forgot to make the verb agree with the subject. Correct the errors.

Moove over, and make room for Maria Gomez! Maria is only ten, but she's already a star! She has been singing and danceing since she was three. Maria live in Los Angeles and likes to spent time with her three cats. Her favorite subject is math

PROOFREADING MARKS

∧ Add
⊙ Add a period
ℓ Take out
↶ Move
≡ Capital letter
/ Small letter
¶ Indent paragraph

Now proofread your biographical sketch. Check your spelling, punctuation, and subject-verb agreement.

A Use the Dictionary: **Pronunciation Key**

Each entry word in a dictionary is followed by its pronunciation. The letters and symbols show how the word is said. Notice that some of the vowels have special marks over them. The pronunciation key tells you what the symbols and marks mean. Here is part of a pronunciation key.

a	add	ā	ace
e	end	ē	equal
i	it	ī	ice
o	odd	ō	open
o͞o	pool	yo͞o	fuse

Use the pronunciation key. Write the spelling for the words in / /.

/mo͞ov/ _____   /hōp/ _____

/skāt/ _____   /wāst ing/ _____

/dans/ _____   /yo͞oz/ _____

B Test Yourself

Use the code to find the missing letters in each word. Write the word.

*= e   # = -ed   @ = -ing

1. us*	6. wast#	11. mov#
2. wast@	7. us#	12. hop*
3. hop#	8. danc@	13. wast*
4. mov@	9. mov*	14. us@
5. danc*	10. hop@	15. danc#

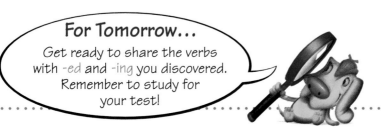

For Tomorrow...
Get ready to share the verbs with -ed and -ing you discovered. Remember to study for your test!

Get Word Wise

A verb with **-ing** can also be an adjective or a noun. Take **dancing**, for example. In this sentence, it's a verb: "Everyone is dancing." Here it's an adjective: "Everyone loved the dancing bear." Here it's a noun: "Dancing is fun for everyone."

Word Study Strategy

See the word

START

Say it slowly

Link sounds and letters

Write

Check

END

Spelling Words

dry	carrying
dried	worry
drying	worried
hurry	worrying
hurried	study *LOOKOUT WORD*
hurrying	studied
carry	studying
carried	

Review	Challenge
waste	replied
gather	replying
play	

My Words

_____

_____

_____

Changing Final **y** to **i**

Ⓐ See and Say

The Spelling Concept

dry + ed = dried

dry + ing = drying

When a verb ends with **y**, change the **y** to **i** before adding **-ed**. Don't change the spelling when you add **-ing**.

Y worry?
I studied!

MEMORY JOGGER

Ⓑ Link Sounds and Letters

Listen as you say the spelling words. They follow the same pattern as **try**, **tried**, **trying**. Write each spelling word in the correct column.

Word Sort

try	tried	trying

Ⓒ Write and Check

Write the two verbs in the poem that are spelling words. Then write each verb with the **-ing** ending and without the ending.

_____ _____

_____ _____

_____ _____

LATE AGAIN!

The little turtle raced and hurried.

He was late and looked so worried.

He came to a stop with a splash and a swish.

"I'd be on time if I were a flying fish!"

Ⓐ Build Vocabulary: **Rhyming Words**

The underlined word in each sentence doesn't fit.
Write the spelling word that rhymes and makes sense.

1. I always <u>muddy</u> at the library.
2. Last night I <u>muddied</u> at home.
3. I <u>scurry</u> that I'll be late.
4. I <u>flurry</u> so I won't be late.
5. My wet coat is <u>trying</u> by the fire.
6. I always <u>marry</u> my lunch to school.
7. I <u>fried</u> my wet shoes in the hot sun.
8. I'm glad my shoes are now <u>try</u>.

Spell Chat
Challenge a classmate to think of another verb that ends with y, and spell it with its -ed and -ing endings.

Ⓑ Word Study: **Word Math**

Add and subtract letters to get different
verb forms. Write each word you make.

9. worry − y + i + ed =
10. study + ing =
11. hurry − y + i + ed =
12. worry + ing =
13. dry − y + i + ed =
14. carry − y + i + ed =
15. hurry + ing =
16. play + ing =

Ⓒ Write

Write two sentences about someone rushing home
from the supermarket. Use these spelling words.

hurrying   carrying   worrying

_____

_____

_____

Be a Spelling Sleuth

Look in the sports pages of your local newspaper for forms of verbs that end with y, such as **carry** and **hurried**. List the words you find.

Spelling Words

dry	carrying
dried	worry
drying	worried
hurry	worrying
hurried	study
hurrying	studied
carry	studying
carried	

Review	Challenge
waste	replied
gather	replying
play	

My Words

_____

_____

_____

_____

Spelling Words

dry	carrying
dried	worry
drying	worried
hurry	worrying
hurried	study LOOKOUT WORD
hurrying	studied
carry	studying
carried	

Review	Challenge
waste	replied
gather	replying
play	

My Words

_____

_____

_____

Quick Write

Write an ad for a new book. Use at least two spelling words.

You may wish to do this activity on a computer.

A Write a Narrative

Imagine that you just met your favorite story character. Who would it be? Write about your meeting. Use two spelling words in your story.

B Proofread

Sandy wrote about meeting Ramona Quimby. She made three spelling errors and one error in punctuation. She also forgot to indent a paragraph. Fix the mistakes.

Tip

When you write, indent the first word of each paragraph.

I just saw Ramona Quimby hurying down Klickitat Street. She was missing a shoe. I ran over and asked what happened Ramona looked worryed. She said that she had lost her sneaker. A big dog had grabbed it. Now she was going to be late for her school pla. Guess what part she had. Cinderella!

PROOFREADING MARKS

∧ Add
⊙ Add a period
ℓ Take out
⊙↗ Move
≡ Capital letter
/ Small letter
¶ Indent paragraph

Now proofread your narrative. Check your spelling and punctuation. Did you indent your paragraph?

Ⓐ Use the Dictionary: **Idioms**

An idiom is a group of words that means something different from what it seems to mean. Read the entry below. **Carry on, carry out,** and **carry the ball** are idioms.

> **car•ry** /ka rē/ *verb*
>
> **1.** To hold onto something and take it somewhere. *Please carry this tray inside.* **2. idiom:** When you **carry on** with something, you continue to do it. **3. idiom:** If you **carry out** a plan or an idea, you put it into practice. **4. idiom:** If you **carry the ball**, you are the one responsible to see that a particular task is done.

Write the idiom that will complete each sentence.

You can count on Jan to _____. She always finishes what she starts.

Dan can _____ the plan for the new park. He knows exactly what to do.

I will _____ with studying. I want to learn my spelling words.

Ⓑ Test Yourself

Figure out the missing letters, and write the spelling words.

1. dr _
2. hurr _ _ _
3. carry_ _ _
4. worry_ _ _
5. stud _ _ _

6. dr _ _ _
7. hurr _
8. carr _ _ _
9. worr_ _ _
10. stud _

11. dry _ _ _
12. hurry_ _ _
13. carr _
14. worr _
15. study_ _ _

For Tomorrow...
Get ready to share the verb forms you have discovered. Remember to study for your test!

Get Word Wise
Did you know that **carry** and **car** are related? They both came from the Latin word **carrus**, which means "vehicle."

Word Study Strategy

See the word

START

Say it slowly

Link sounds and letters

Write

Check

END

What's the Message?

Complete each sentence with a spelling word from the box.

> afternoon hoping worry hurry homework

It was Friday (1) and Emily was on her way home from school. She was in a (2) to get home. She had (3) to do, and she was (4) to finish it before supper. She didn't want to (5) about school work tomorrow, because tomorrow would be a very special day.

> what's it's almost studying sidewalk

She was (6) home when she saw something written in chalk on the (7). It said: IBQQZCJSUIEBZ, FNJMZ. She was (8) the strange message when her friend Roberto came by.

"Hi, (9) that?" asked Roberto.

"Some kind of message," said Emily. "I think (10) in code."

> grinning hoped began I've birthday

Roberto (11) he could figure out the code. He pulled a pencil and pad out of his backpack and (12) to write. All of a sudden he said, " (13) got it! Replace each letter in the message with the letter that comes before it in the alphabet."

"Right!" Emily said (14). "It says: Happy (15), Emily!"

IBQQZ
CJSUI
EBZ,
FNJMZ

You're Invited

In each sentence, write the contraction for the underlined words.

1. Have you heard that <u>there is</u> something special happening? _____

2. Well, <u>here is</u> what it is. _____

3. <u>I am</u> having a party. _____

4. I know <u>it is</u> going to be great. _____

5. It will be even better if <u>you are</u> there. _____

6. <u>I have</u> invited all our friends. _____

7. I hope you <u>do not</u> have other plans. _____

8. <u>I will</u> be so disappointed if you can't come. _____

9. I hope <u>we will</u> see you! _____

don't	it's
we'll	I'll
I'm	you're
I've	here's
there's	

Word Clues

swimming   dancing   barefoot

downstairs   sidewalk

Write the spelling word that goes with each clue.

10. not wearing shoes and socks _____

11. moving to music _____

12. moving through the water _____

13. opposite of upstairs _____

14. a path along the street _____

Double the Compounds

Make compound words. The two words you see share a word. The missing word ends the first word and begins the second word. Write the missing word as shown in the example.

back<u>yard</u>stick

rail_____way

pop_____flower

tip_____nail

out_____walk

home_____out

Lesson 36 Review

begin	sunshine
barefoot	hope
swim	afternoon
move	used
don't	study
I'll	backyard
dance	didn't
can't	

Tip
Remember to put the apostrophe in contractions.

Fun All Year Round

What do you like to do during the year? Do you like sports? reading? going places? Finish each sentence. Use two or more spelling words.

1. In June, I like to

_____

2. Last summer, I

_____

3. Fall is a good time to

_____

4. In November, I might

_____

5. In the spring, I always

_____

Look back at My Words and the words you misspelled in your Unit 6 Posttests. Use some of them to write about your favorite time of year.

_____

_____

Summer Plans

Write a paragraph about something you want to do this summer. Proofread your work for spelling, capitalization, and punctuation.

_____

_____

PROOFREADING MARKS
∧ Add
⊙ Add a period
ℓ Take out
⤳ Move
≡ Capital letter
/ Small letter
¶ Indent paragraph

Stair Steps

Read each definition, and write the base word on the top step. Then complete the word family by adding **-ed** and **-ing**. Write the words on the other steps.

hope	moved	hoping	move
hurried	dance	moving	hurrying
dancing	hurry	danced	hoped

EXAMPLE:

put to work

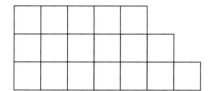

u	s	e		
u	s	e	d	
u	s	i	n	g

Spelling Matters!

1. move to music

2. go to another place

3. wish for

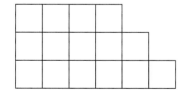

4. rush

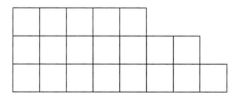

A B C D E F G H I
J K L M N O P Q R
S T U V W X Y Z
a b c d e f g h i j
k l m n o p q r s t
u v w x y z

A B C D E F G H I
J K L M N O P Q R
S T U V W X Y Z
a b c d e f g h i j
k l m n o p q r s t
u v w x y z

about	catch	girl	machine	studying
above	change	guess	more	swimming
across	children	gym	morning	teacher
afternoon	choice	hear	mother	tear
again	choose	heard	moving	their
almost	circle	heart	near	there's
along	color	here's	nothing	they're
another	dear	hurried	orange	think
April	didn't	hurt	party	together
August	don't	I'll	purple	used
aunt	downstairs	I'm	right	wear
backyard	early	it's	sandwich	we'll
balloon	earth	I've	saw	were
because	everywhere	January	sent	what's
before	father	just	stopped	won't
beginning	fault	key	store	world
birthday	February	large	straight	worried
bother	first	learn	stretch	write
break	four	loose	strong	you're
can't	friend	lose	studied	you've

You will find all your spelling words in
alphabetical order in the Spelling Dictionary.
Look at the sample entry below to see how to use it.

The **entry word** is the word
you look up. This shows how
it is divided into syllables.

This part tells you
how to **pronounce**
the entry word.

wa·ter /wô tər/

1. *noun* The liquid that falls as rain and fills oceans, rivers, and lakes.

2. *verb* To pour water on.

▶ *verb* **watering, watered**

These are **other forms** of the entry word.

Look here to find the **meaning** of the word. This entry word has two meanings, one when it is used as a noun and one when it is used as a verb.

a·bout /ə bout/
1. *preposition* On a certain subject.
2. *adverb* More or less.

a·bove /ə buv/ *preposition*
1. Higher up than, or over.
2. More than.

a·cross /ə krôs/ *preposition*
1. From one side to the other.
2. On the other side.

af·ter·noon /af tər no͞on/
noun The time of day between noon and evening.

a·gain /ə gen/ *adverb*
One more time.

age /āj/
1. *noun* The number of years a person has lived. 2. *verb* To become older.
▶ *verb* **aging, aged**

a·go /ə gō/ *adverb*
In the past; before now.

a·gree /ə grē/ *verb*
To say yes to something.

air /âr/
1. *noun* The invisible mixture of gases a person breathes.

air·plane /âr plān/ *noun*
A flying machine with wings and an engine.

air·port /âr pôrt/ *noun*
A place where airplanes take off and land.

a·like /ə līk/
1. *adjective* Looking or acting the same. 2. *adverb* In a similar way.

a·live /ə līv/ *adjective*
1. Living. 2. Full of life.

al·most /ôl mōst/ *adverb*
Very nearly.

a·lone /ə lōn/ *adjective*
Without anyone else.

a·long /ə lông/ *preposition*
Following the length or direction of something.

a·long·side /ə lông sīd/
1. *adverb* At the side.
2. *preposition* By the side of.

an·nu·al /an yo͞o əl/ *adjective*
Happening once a year.

an·oth·er /ə nuth ər/
1. *adjective* One more of the same kind. 2. *pronoun* A different one.

Spelling Dictionary

ap·pear /ə pēr/ *verb*
1. To come into view. 2. To seem.

A·pril /ā prəl/ *noun*
The fourth month of the year.

Word History

April may have come from the name for the Greek goddess of love, Aphrodite. Some people, however, think April comes from the Latin word "to open," because flower buds open in the spring.

arm /ärm/
1. *noun* The body part between your shoulder and hand. 2. *verb* To get ready for war by taking up weapons.

Au·gust /ô gəst/ *noun*
The eighth month of the year.

aunt /ant *or* änt/ *noun*
The sister of one's father or mother; the wife of one's uncle.

au·thor /ô thər/ *noun*
A person who writes a book, play, or article.

au·tumn /ô təm/ *noun*
The season between summer and winter.
Synonym: fall

aw·ful /ô fəl/ *adjective*
1. Terrible. 2. *(informal)* Very great.

ba·by-sit·ting /bā bē si ting/ *noun*
The act of staying with and looking after children.

back /bak/
1. *noun* The rear part of your body between the neck and the end of your spine. 2. *noun* The end or side opposite the front. 3. *adverb* Where someone or something was before. 4. *verb* To support.

back·yard /bak yärd/ *noun*
An open area behind a house.

bal·loon /bə lōōn/ *noun*
A small bag made of thin rubber that is blown up and used as a decoration.

band·age /ban dij/
1. *noun* A piece of material that is wrapped around an injured part of the body to protect it. 2. *verb* To put a bandage on.

bare·foot /bâr fōōt/
adjective Without shoes and socks.

bath /bath/ *noun*
1. The act of washing something in water. 2. The water used for bathing.

beach /bēch/ *noun*
A place where land and water meet, often covered with sand. *plural* **beaches**

bear /bâr/ *noun*
A large, heavy animal with thick fur.

be·cause /bi kôz/ *conjunction*
For the reason or reasons that.

be·come /bi kum/ *verb*
1. To start to be. 2. To look good on.
▶becoming, became

be·fore /bi fôr/ *preposition* Sooner.

be·fore·hand /bi fôr hand/ *adverb*
Ahead of time.

be·gan /bi gan/ *verb*
Past tense of **begin**. Started.

be·gin /bi gin/ *verb*
To start. ▶beginning, began, begun

be·gin·ning /bi gin ing/
1. *verb* Starting. 2. *noun* The first part.

be·hind /bi hīnd/ *preposition*
On the other side; toward the back.

be·long /bi long/ *verb*
To be a part of something.

be·low /bi lō/
1. *preposition* Lower than. 2. *adverb* In or to a lower place, as in *The sun sank below the horizon.*

bench /bench/ *noun*
A long, narrow seat.

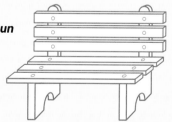

be·side /bi sīd/ *preposition* Next to.

be·tween /bi twēn/ *preposition*
To be in the middle of two things.

bird /bûrd/ *noun*
A creature with two legs, wings, feathers, and a beak. Most birds can fly.

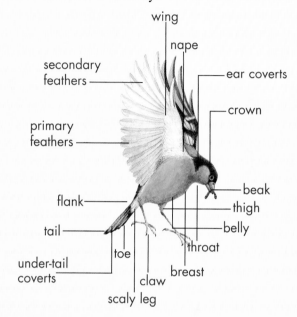

wing
nape
secondary feathers
ear coverts
crown
primary feathers
flank
beak
thigh
belly
tail
throat
under-tail coverts
toe
breast
claw
scaly leg

birth·day /bûrth dā/ *noun*
1. The day that someone was born.
2. The yearly celebration of someone's birth.

black /blak/ *adjective*
The color of the dark sky at night.

blame /blām/ *verb*
To say something is another person's fault.

blind /blīnd/ *adjective* Unable to see.

a	add	ô	order	ŧh	this
ā	ace	o͞o	took	zh	vision
â	care	o͞o	pool		
ä	palm	u	up		
e	end	û	burn		
ē	equal	yo͞o	fuse	ə	=
i	it	oi	oil	a	in *above*
ī	ice	ou	pout	e	in *sicken*
o	odd	ng	ring	i	in *possible*
ō	open	th	thin	o	in *melon*
				u	in *circus*

blink /blingk/ *verb*
To close and open your eyes very quickly.

block /blok/ *noun*
1. A piece of something that is hard.
2. The distance from one street to the next.

boil /boil/ *verb*
To heat a liquid until it bubbles.

born /bôrn/ *adjective* Brought into life.

both·er /both ər/ *verb* To annoy.

boy /boi/ *noun* A male child.

brain /brān/ *noun*
1. The organ inside your head that controls your body and thinking. 2. Your mind.

break /brāk/ *verb*
1. To damage something so it no longer works.
2. To do something that you shouldn't do, as in *break a rule.* ▶ **broke, broken**

break·fast /brek fəst/ *noun*
The first meal of the day.

breeze /brēz/ *noun*
A gentle wind.

bridge /brij/ *noun*
A structure built over a river or road so that people can get from one side to the other.

brush /brush/ *noun*
An object used for sweeping, painting, or smoothing hair. *plural* **brushes**

budge /buj/ *verb*
To move something just a bit.
▶ **budging, budged**

bunk /bungk/ *noun*
A narrow bed.

 C c

cage /kāj/ *noun*
A place where animals or birds are kept.

cal·en·dar /kal ən dər/ *noun*
A chart that shows the days, weeks, and months in a year.

cam·er·a /kam ər ə/ *noun*
1. A machine for taking photographs or making films. 2. A device for transmitting images of a television broadcast.

camp /kamp/ *noun*
An outdoor area with tents or cabins where people stay for short visits.

can't /kant/ *contraction*
A short form of *cannot.*

car /kär/ *noun*
A motor vehicle with four wheels that carries passengers.

care /kâr/ *verb*
To be concerned about something.
▶ **caring, cared**

car·pen·ter /kär pən tər/ *noun*
Someone who works with wood or builds and repairs the wooden part of buildings.

car·ried /ka rēd/ *verb*
Past tense of **carry.** Held on to something and took it somewhere.

car·ry /ka rē/ *verb*
To hold onto something and take it somewhere.

car·ry·ing /ka rē ing/ *verb*
Holding onto something and taking it somewhere.

catch /kach/ *verb*
To grab hold of something.
▶ **catches, catching, caught**

cat·sup /kat sup or kech up/ *noun*
A thick sauce made with tomatoes and spices. Also spelled **ketchup.**

Word History

Both *catsup* and *ketchup* come from the Chinese term *ke-tsiap,* or "fish sauce." The original catsup did not include tomatoes as an ingredient. American sailors were the first to add them to an early type of catsup that the British made from mushrooms.

cave /kāv/ *noun*
A large hole in the ground or in the side of a hill.

cel·e·brate /sel ə brāt/ *verb*
To do something you enjoy on a special occasion. ▶ **celebrating, celebrated**

cell /sel/ *noun*
1. A small room. **2.** A very small part of a person, animal, or plant. **Cell** sounds like **sell.**

cent /sent/ *noun*
A unit of money. **Cent** sounds like **scent** and **sent.**

cen·ter /sen tər/ *noun*
The middle of something.

chair /châr/ *noun*
A piece of furniture you sit on, with a seat, legs, and back.

chal·lenge /chal ənj/
noun Something that is difficult or that takes extra work to do.

change /chānj/
1. *verb* To become or make different. **2.** *noun* Coins. **3.** *noun* The money you get back if you pay more than something costs.

chap·ter /chap tər/ *noun*
One of the parts into which a book is divided.

a	add	ô	order	ŧħ	this
ā	ace	o͞o	took	zh	vision
â	care	o͞o	pool		
ä	palm	u	up		
e	end	û	burn		
ē	equal	yo͞o	fuse	ə	=
i	it	oi	oil	a	in *above*
ī	ice	ou	pout	e	in *sicken*
o	odd	ng	ring	i	in *possible*
ō	open	th	thin	o	in *melon*
				u	in *circus*

check /chek/
1. *verb* To look at something to make sure it is all right. 2. *noun* A pattern of squares of different colors.

check·ers /chek ərz/ *noun*
A board game for two players.

chick·en /chik ən/ *noun*
1. A bird that is raised on a farm for its eggs and meat. 2. The meat from this bird used as food.

child /chīld/ *noun*
1. A young boy or girl. 2. A son or daughter. *plural* **children**

chil·dren /chil drən/ *noun, plural*
Plural form of **child**; young boys and girls.

chin /chin/ *noun*
The part of your face below the mouth.

choice /chois/ *noun*
The thing or person that has been selected.

choose /chōōz/ *verb*
1. To pick out one person or thing from several. 2. To decide. ▶**chose, choosing, chosen**

cho·rus /kôr əs/ *noun*
1. The part of a song that is repeated after each verse. 2. A large group of people who sing together. *plural* **choruses**

chuck·le /chuk əl/ *verb*
To laugh quietly. ▶**chuckling, chuckled**

cir·cle /sûr kəl/ *noun*
A flat, perfectly round shape.

cir·cus /sûr kəs/ *noun*
A show in which clowns, acrobats, and animals perform.

ci·ty /sit ē/ *noun*
A very large or important town. *plural* **cities**

clear /klir/ *adjective*
Easy to see through.

clock /klok/ *noun*
A device that tells the time.

cloud /kloud/ *noun*
A white or gray puffy-looking group of water drops suspended in the sky.

club /klub/ *noun*
A group of people who meet regularly to share a common interest.

coach /kōch/
1. *verb* To help someone in a sport or subject. 2. *noun* A person who does this.

co·coon /kə kōōn/ *noun*
A silky covering that some animals make for protection.

col·lege /kol ij/ *noun*
A place where students continue to study after high school.

col·or /kul ər/
1. *noun* Wavelengths of light that bounce off an object and are perceived as red, yellow, and so on. 2. *verb* To make something red, yellow, and so on.

con·test /kon test/ *noun*
An activity in which one person or team tries to do better than another.

cool /kōōl/ *adjective*
Rather cold.

cor·ner /kôr nər/ *noun*
The place where two sides of something or two streets meet.

cost /kost or kôst/ *verb*
To have a certain price.

couch /kouch/ *noun*
A long, soft piece of furniture for sitting or lying.

crab /krab/ *noun*
A creature that lives in water and has a hard shell, eight legs, and two claws.

crawl /krôl/ *verb*
1. To move on your hands and knees.
2. To move slowly.

creek /krēk/ *noun* A small stream.

crick·et /krik it/ *noun*
A jumping insect that is like a grasshopper.

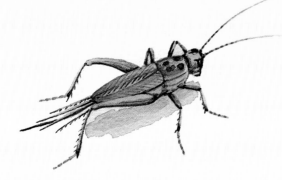

croak /krōk/ *verb*
To make a deep, hoarse sound, like that of a frog.

cross /krôs/ *verb*
To go from one side to the other.

crunch /krunch/ *verb*
To chew noisily.

cub /kub/ *noun*
A young animal, such as a lion or bear.

cup·board /kub ərd/ *noun*
A place for storing food, dishes, or other things.

 D d

dance /dans/ *verb*
To move in time to music. ▶**dancing, danced**

danced /danst/ *verb*
Past tense of **dance**. Moved in time to music.

danc·ing /dan sing/ *verb*
Moving in time to music.

dare /dâr/ *verb*
To ask someone to do something that may be hard or dangerous. ▶**daring, dared**

dark /därk/
1. *adjective* Without light. 2. *noun* Nightfall.

dawn /dôn/ *noun*
The start of the day; sunrise.

dear /dēr/ *adjective*
Much loved.

a	add	ô	order	th	this
ā	ace	oo	took	zh	vision
â	care	ōō	pool		
ä	palm	u	up		
e	end	û	burn	ə	=
ē	equal	yōō	fuse	a	in *above*
i	it	oi	oil	e	in *sicken*
ī	ice	ou	pout	i	in *possible*
o	odd	ng	ring	o	in *melon*
ō	open	th	thin	u	in *circus*

De·cem·ber /di sem bər/ *noun*
The twelfth month of the year.

did·n't /did ənt/ *contraction*
A short form of *did not.*

die /dī/ *verb*
To stop living. ▶**dying, died**

ditch /dich/ *noun*
A long, narrow trench in the ground.
plural **ditches**

don't /dōnt/ *contraction*
A short form of *do not.*

door /dôr/ *noun*
A barrier that opens and closes at the entrance or exit of a building or room.

down·stairs /doun stârz/ *adverb*
Down the stairs or to a lower floor.

draw /drô/ *verb*
To make a picture with a pencil, pen, or similar tool.

dried /drīd/ *verb*
Past tense of **dry**. Took the moisture out of something.

drift /drift/ *verb*
1. To move wherever the wind or water takes an object. **2.** To move with no purpose.

drink /dringk/
1. *noun* A liquid that you swallow. **2.** *verb* To swallow liquid. ▶*verb* **drinking, drank, drunk**

drive /drīv/ *verb*
To run and control a vehicle.
▶**driving, drove, driven**

dry /drī/
1. *verb* To take the moisture out of something.
2. *adjective* Not wet. ▶*verb* **drying, dried**

dry·ing /drī ing/ *verb*
Taking the moisture out of something.

E e

ear /ēr/ *noun*
1. The part of the body used for hearing.
2. A part of some plants on which grain or seeds grow, such as *an ear of corn.*

ear·ly /ûr lē/
1. *adverb* At the beginning.
2. *adjective* Before the usual time.

earn /ûrn/ *verb*
To get money or a reward for work you do.

earth /ûrth/ *noun*
1. The planet on which we live. **2.** Soil.

earth·quake /ûrth kwāk/ *noun* A sudden, strong shaking of the earth that happens when the earth's crust moves.

edge /ej/ *noun*
1. A boundary. **2.** The sharp side of a cutting tool.

en·joy /en joi/ *verb*
To get pleasure from doing something.

everywhere /ev rē hwâr/ *adverb*
In all places.

ex·haust·ed /ig zôst əd/ *adjective*
Feeling very tired or weak.

fair /fâr/
1. *adjective* Reasonable. 2. *adjective* Neither good nor bad. 3. *noun* An outdoor show, often with animals.

fair·y /fâr ē/ *noun*
A character in a tale. *plural* **fairies**

far /fär/
1. *adverb* A great distance. *Have you traveled far?*
2. *adjective* Distant; not near.

farm /färm/
1. *verb* To grow crops and raise animals.
2. *noun* A place where crops are grown and animals are raised.

fash·ion /fash ən/ *noun* Clothing that is popular at a certain time.

fa·ther /fä thər/ *noun*
A male parent.

fault /fôlt/ *noun*
Something that is wrong, often that someone is to blame for.

fear /fēr/ *noun*
The feeling you have when you are afraid or think that something bad may happen.

feath·er /feth ər/ *noun*
One of the light, fluffy parts that covers a bird's body.

Feb·ru·ar·y /feb rōō er ē or feb yōō er ē/ *noun* The second month of the year.

find /fīnd/ *verb*
To discover or come across something.
▶**finding, found**

fin·ger /fing gər/ *noun*
One of the five long parts of your hand that you can move.

fin·ish /fin ish/ *verb*
To end or complete something.

first /fûrst/ *adjective*
That which comes earliest; before second.

flash /flash/ *noun*
1. A short burst of light.
2. A very brief period of time.

flight /flīt/ *noun*
1. The act of flying or moving through the air.
2. A trip by aircraft.

floor /flôr/ *noun*
1. The flat surface that you walk or stand on inside a building. 2. A story in a building.

a	add	ô	order	th	this
ā	ace	oo	took	zh	vision
â	care	oo	pool		
ä	palm	u	up		
e	end	û	burn	ə	=
ē	equal	yoo	fuse	a	in *above*
i	it	oi	oil	e	in *sicken*
ī	ice	ou	pout	i	in *possible*
o	odd	ng	ring	o	in *melon*
ō	open	th	thin	u	in *circus*

flow·er /flou ər/ *noun*
The colored part of a plant that makes seeds or fruit.

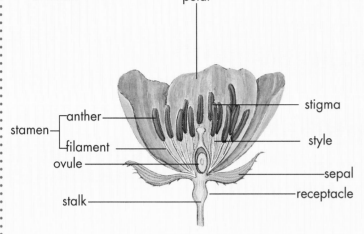

petal

stamen — anther
        filament
ovule
stalk

stigma
style
sepal
receptacle

flute /flo͞ot/ *noun*
A long, thin musical instrument with an airhole.

fool /fo͞ol/ *noun*
A person who doesn't have good sense.

for /fôr/ *preposition*
1. Meaning to be used on or with. 2. Meeting the needs of. 3. Over the time or distance of. 4. Due to.

for·est /fôr ist *or* for ist/ *noun*
A large area covered with many trees and plants.

four /fôr/ *noun*
The number, written 4, that comes between three and five.

freck·les /frek əlz/ *noun, plural*
Small, light brown spots on a person's skin.

friend /frend/ *noun*
Someone whom you know well and enjoy being with.

fright·en /frīt ən/ *verb* To scare someone.

front /frunt/ *noun*
The part of something that comes first.

fudge /fuj/ *noun*
A candy made with butter, milk, sugar, and usually chocolate.

fur·ni·ture /fûr ni chər/ *noun*
The movable things like chairs, tables, and beds in a home or office.

G g

game /gām/ *noun*
1. An activity with rules that can be played by one or more people. 2. Wild animals.

ga·rage /gə räzh *or* gə räj/ *noun*
A building used to park or store cars and other vehicles.

gar·bage /gär bij/ *noun*
Things that are thrown away.

gar·den /gär dən/ *noun*
A place where flowers or other plants are grown.

gas /gas/ *noun*
1. A substance like air that will spread to fill a space. 2. A liquid fuel used in many vehicles. *Gas* is short for *gasoline*.

gate /gāt/ *noun*
A frame or barrier at an entrance that can be opened and closed.

gath·er /gath ər/ *verb*
1. To pick up and collect things. 2. To come together in a group.

gave /gāv/ *verb*
Past tense of **give**. Handed something to another person. ▶give, giving

geese /gēs/ *noun, plural*
Plural form of **goose**. A bird with a long neck and webbed feet.

gen·e·ral /jen ər əl/
1. *adjective* To do with everybody or everything; not specialized. **2.** *noun* A high-ranking officer in the army, air force, or marines.

gen·tle /jen təl/ *adjective*
1. Not rough. **2.** Kind.

gi·ant /jī ənt/
1. *noun* A very large person, usually in fairy tales. **2.** *adjective* Very large. ▶ *Synonyms: enormous, gigantic, huge*

gi·gan·tic /jī gan tik/ *adjective*
Huge.

gig·gle /gig əl/ *verb*
To laugh in a silly or nervous way.
▶ **giggling, giggled**

gig·gling /gig ling/ *verb*
Laughing in a silly or nervous way.

gi·raffe /jə raf/ *noun*
An African animal with a very long neck and long legs.

girl /gûrl/ *noun*
A female child.

glass /glas/ *noun*
1. A transparent material used for windows, bottles, and eyeglasses. **2.** A container for drinking. *plural* **glasses**

gloves /gluvz/ *noun, plural*
Hand coverings worn for warmth or protection.

goose /gōōs/ *noun*
A large bird with a long neck and webbed feet.
plural **geese**

grand /grand/ *adjective*
Large or wonderful.

grass·hop·per /gras hop ər/ *noun*
An insect that eats plants and leaps with its long back legs.

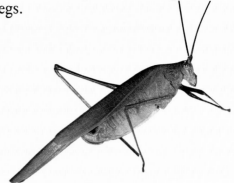

grin /grin/
1. *verb* To give a big smile. **2.** *noun* The smile itself. ▶ *verb* **grinning, grinned**

grind /grīnd/ *verb*
To crush something into powder.
▶ **grinding, ground**

grinned /grind/ *verb*
Past tense of **grin**. Gave a big smile.

grin·ning /grin ing/ *verb*
Giving a big smile.

grouch·y /grouch ē/ *adjective*
Mean or nasty.

ground /ground/ *noun*
The surface of the earth.

guard /gärd/
1. *verb* To protect or watch over a person or place. **2.** *noun* Someone who protects a person or place.

a	add	ô	order	ŧħ	this
ā	ace	ōō	took	zh	vision
â	care	ōō	pool		
ä	palm	u	up		
e	end	û	burn	ə	=
ē	equal	yōō	fuse	a	in *above*
i	it	oi	oil	e	in *sicken*
ī	ice	ou	pout	i	in *possible*
o	odd	ng	ring	o	in *melon*
ō	open	th	thin	u	in *circus*

guard·i·an /gär dē ən/ *noun*
Someone who legally looks after a child but who is not the parent of the child.

guess /ges/ *verb*
To give an answer without being sure that the answer is right.

guest /gest/ *noun*
1. Someone who has been invited to visit or to stay in someone else's home. **2.** Someone staying in a hotel or motel.

guide /gīd/ *verb*
To help people, usually by showing them around a place. ▶**guiding, guided**

gum /gum/
1. *noun* The pink area around your teeth.
2. A sweet substance used for chewing.

guy /gī/ *noun*
A man or a boy.

gym /jim/ *noun*
A large room or building with special equipment that is used for exercise or sports.
Gym is short for *gymnasium*.

hair /hâr/ *noun*
The mass of soft strands that grow on the heads and bodies of people and animals.

hard /härd/ *adjective*
1. Not soft. **2.** Difficult. **3.** Acting with energy, as in *a hard worker*.

haul /hôl/ *verb*
To pull something with difficulty.
▶**hauling, hauled**

heal /hēl/ *verb*
To cure someone or make the person healthy.
Heal sounds like **heel**.

hear /hēr/ *verb*
To sense sounds through your ears.
▶**hearing, heard**

heard /hûrd/ *verb*
Past tense of **hear**. Sensed sounds through your ears.

heart /härt/ *noun*
The organ in your chest that pumps blood all through your body.

heel /hēl/ *noun*
The back part of your foot. **Heel** sounds like **heal**.

here's /hērz/ *contraction*
A short form of *here is*.

home·work /hōm wûrk/ *noun*
Work assigned at school that is to be done at home.

hope /hōp/
1. *verb* To wish for something. **2.** *noun* A feeling of expecting or wanting something.
▶ *verb* **hoping, hoped**

hoped /hōpt/ *verb*
Past tense of **hope**. Wished for something.

hop·ing /hōp ing/ *verb*
Wishing for something.

hur·ried /hûr ēd/ *verb*
Past tense of **hurry**. Did things as fast as possible.

hur·ry /hûr ē/ *verb*
To do things as fast as possible.
▶ **hurrying, hurried**

hur·ry·ing /hûr ē ing/ *verb*
Doing things as fast as possible.

hurt /hûrt/ *verb*
1. To cause pain. **2.** To be in pain.
▶ **hurting, hurt**

I'll /īl/ *contraction*
A short form of *I will* or *I shall*.

I'm /īm/ *contraction* A short form of *I am*.

I've /īv/ *contraction* A short form of *I have*.

it's /its/ *contraction*
A short form of *it is* or *it has*.

itch /ich/
1. *verb* To scratch your skin because it feels uncomfortable. **2.** *noun* The sensation that causes you to itch.

J j

jack·et /jak it/ *noun*
A short coat.

Jan·u·ar·y /jan yōō er ē/ *noun*
The first month of the year.

jar /jär/ *noun*
A container with a wide opening.

jeans /jēnz/ *noun, plural*
Pants made from denim cloth.

a	add	ô	order	ŧh	this
ā	ace	ōō	took	zh	vision
â	care	ōō	pool		
ä	palm	u	up		
e	end	û	burn	ə	=
ē	equal	yōō	fuse	a	in *above*
i	it	oi	oil	e	in *sicken*
ī	ice	ou	pout	i	in *possible*
o	odd	ng	ring	o	in *melon*
ō	open	th	thin	u	in *circus*

jel·ly /jel ē/ *noun*
A sweet, thick food made from boiled fruit and sugar.

jet /jet/ *noun*
An aircraft powered by jet engines.

job /job/ *noun*
1. A task or chore. **2.** The work that someone does for a living.

join /join/ *verb*
To fasten two things together.

joke /jōk/
1. *verb* To say or do funny things so other people will laugh. **2.** *noun* A short story with a funny ending. ▶ *verb* **joking, joked**

joy /joi/ *noun*
A feeling of great happiness.

judge /juj/
1. *noun* A person who listens to cases in court and decides the punishment for guilty people.
2. *verb* To decide.

Ju·ly /jōō lī *or* jə lī/ *noun*
The seventh month of the year.

jump /jump/ *verb*
1. To push off with your legs and feet and move into and through the air. **2.** To get up suddenly.
3. *idiom* **Jump for joy** means "to be very happy."

June /jōōn/ *noun*
The sixth month of the year.

jun·gle /jung gəl/ *noun*
Land in warm areas near the equator that is thickly covered with trees and vines.

just /just/
1. *adjective* Fair. **2.** *adverb* A very little while ago.
3. *adverb* Exactly.

K k

kan·ga·roo /kang gə rōō/ *noun*
An animal from Australia with short front legs and long, powerful back legs for leaping. The female carries her young in a pouch.

keep /kēp/ *verb*
1. To have something and not get rid of it.
2. To stay the same. **3.** To continue doing something. **4.** To store.

ketch·up /kech up/ *noun*
A thick sauce made with tomatoes and spices.
Also spelled **catsup**.

key /kē/ *noun*
1. A piece of metal made to fit into a lock to open it. **2.** A button on a computer or typewriter.

kids /kidz/ *noun, plural (informal)*
Children.

kind /kīnd/
1. *adjective* Helpful; sensitive to another person's needs. **2.** *noun* A group of the same type of things, as in *A rose is one kind of flower.*

kin·der·gar·ten /kin dər gär tən/ *noun*
A class for children ages four to six.

Word History

Kindergarten is the German word for "children's garden." The first kindergarten was opened in Germany in 1837 by Friedrich Wilhelm August Froebel. Froebel, who had an unhappy childhood, spent his life opening schools where children could play and explore the world.

---

kind·ness /kīnd nis/ *noun*
The quality of being kind.

kiss /kis/
1. *verb* To touch with the lips to show you like someone. **2.** *noun* A touch with the lips.

kitch·en /kich ən/ *noun*
A room where food is prepared.

kite /kīt/ *noun*
A light frame covered with paper or material that is attached to a long string and flown in the wind.

kit·ten /kit ən/ *noun*
A young cat.

L l

lan·guage /lang gwij/ *noun*
The words people use to talk and write.

large /lärj/ *adjective*
Great in size or amount.
Synonyms: huge, big, gigantic

launch /lônch/ *verb*
1. To put a boat in the water. **2.** To send a rocket into space. **3.** To start something new.

a	add	ô	order	ŧħ	this
ā	ace	o͝o	took	zh	vision
â	care	o͞o	pool		
ä	palm	u	up		
e	end	û	burn	ə	=
ē	equal	yo͞o	fuse	a	in *above*
i	it	oi	oil	e	in *sicken*
ī	ice	ou	pout	i	in *possible*
o	odd	ng	ring	o	in *melon*
ō	open	th	thin	u	in *circus*

lawn /lôn/ *noun*
An area covered with grass, usually around a house.

leak /lēk/ *verb*
To have liquid or gas run out from its container.

learn /lûrn/ *verb*
1. To gain knowledge or a skill. **2.** To memorize.
3. To discover some news.

ledge /lej/ *noun*
1. A narrow shelf that sticks out from a wall.
2. A narrow shelf on the side of a mountain.

lie /lī/
1. *verb* To get in a flat, horizontal position.
▶ *verb* **lying, lay 2.** *verb* To say something that is not true. ▶ *verb* **lying, lied 3.** *noun* A statement that is not true.

lock /lok/
1. *verb* To fasten something with a key.
2. *noun* A part of a door that you open and shut with a key.

long /lông/
1. *adjective* More than the average length.
2. From one end to the other. **3.** Taking a lot of time. *Antonym: short*

loose /lōōs/
1. *adjective* Not attached firmly. **2.** Free.
3. Not fitting tightly.

lose /lōōz/ *verb*
To misplace or fail to keep something.
▶ **losing, lost**

loy·al·ty /loi əl tē/ *noun*
The quality of being faithful to friends or beliefs.

M m

ma·chine /mə shēn/ *noun*
A piece of equipment that has moving parts and is used to do jobs.

main /mān/ *adjective*
Most important. **Main** sounds like **mane**.

man·age /man ij/ *verb*
1. To be in charge of a store or business.
2. To be able to do something that is difficult.
▶ **managing, managed**

mane /mān/ *noun*
The long, thick hair on the head and neck of a horse or lion. **Mane** sounds like **main**.

march /märch/
1. *verb* To walk together with even, regular steps.
2. *noun* A piece of music people march to.

March /märch/ *noun*
The third month of the year.

mark /märk/ *noun*
1. A small scratch or stain. 2. A written sign, such as a question mark.

match /mach/
1. *noun* A small, thin piece of wood or cardboard with a chemical tip that is struck to make a flame. 2. *verb* To go well with, as in *colors that match*.

May /mā/ *noun*
The fifth month of the year.

mild /mīld/ *adjective*
1. Not too harsh. 2. Gentle.

mind /mīnd/
1. *noun* The part of you that thinks, feels, and understands. 2. *verb* To look after someone or something. 3. *verb* To care or be bothered about something.

month /munth/ *noun*
One of the 12 time periods that make up a year.

month·ly /munth lē/
1. *adjective* Happening every month, as in *a monthly trip*. 2. *adverb* Once a month, as in *I write my grandfather monthly*.

moose /mōos/ *noun*
A large animal of the deer family. The male has large antlers.

more /môr/
1. *adjective* Greater in number or size. 2. *adjective* Extra or additional. 3. *adverb* To a greater degree, as in *Please be more careful*.

morn·ing /môr ning/ *noun*
The time of day between midnight and noon or sunrise and noon.

moth·er /muth ər/ *noun*
A female parent.

move /mōov/
1. *verb* To change place or position. 2. *verb* To change where you live or work. 3. *noun* A step or a change in position. ▶ *verb* moving, moved

a	add	ô	order	th	this
ā	ace	ōō	took	zh	vision
â	care	ōō	pool		
ä	palm	u	up		
e	end	û	burn	ə	=
ē	equal	yōō	fuse	a	in *above*
i	it	oi	oil	e	in *sicken*
ī	ice	ou	pout	i	in *possible*
o	odd	ng	ring	o	in *melon*
ō	open	th	thin	u	in *circus*

moved /mo͞ovd/ *verb*
Past tense of **move**. Changed place or position.

mov·ing /mo͞ov ing/ *verb*
Changing place or position.

mule /myo͞ol/ *noun*
An animal whose mother is a horse and father is a donkey.

mu·sic /myo͞o zik/ *noun*
1. A pleasant pattern of sounds, such as in a song. **2.** Printed or written notes that stand for musical sounds.

N n

near /nēr/
1. *preposition* Close to. **2.** *adverb* Close. **3.** *verb* To come closer to something. **4.** *adjective* Narrow or close.

neck /nek/ *noun*
The part of your body that joins your head to your shoulders.

noise /noiz/ *noun*
A loud sound, usually unpleasant.

noon /no͞on/ *noun*
Twelve o'clock in the middle of the day.

noth·ing /nuth ing/
1. *pronoun* Not anything at all. **2.** *pronoun* Not anything important. **3.** *noun* Zero.

No·vem·ber /nō vem bər/ *noun*
The eleventh month of the year.

nurse /nûrs/
1. *noun* A person who looks after people who are sick, usually in a hospital. **2.** *verb* To treat with care. ▶ *verb* **nursing, nursed**

O o

oak /ōk/ *noun*
A large hardwood tree that produces acorns.

Oc·to·ber /ok tō bər/ *noun*
The tenth month of the year.

oil /oil/
1. *noun* A thick, greasy liquid. **2.** *verb* To cover or fill something with oil.

or·ange /ôr inj *or* or inj/
1. *noun* The color made by mixing red and yellow. **2.** *adjective* As in *orange sneakers*. **3.** *noun* A round citrus fruit.

or·ches·tra /ôr kə strə/ *noun*
A large group of musicians who play their instruments together.

os·trich /os trich/ *noun*
A large bird that can run very fast but cannot fly.

oth·er /utħ ər/ *adjective*
1. Different; not the same. **2.** More or extra.

oy·ster /oi stər/ *noun*
A flat shellfish that has a shell made up of two hinged parts.

pack /pak/
1. *verb* To put things in a box or other container. **2.** *noun* A sturdy carrying bag.

page /pāj/ *noun*
One side of a sheet of paper, as in a book or newspaper.

pair /pâr/ *noun*
1. Two things that match or go together. **2.** One thing that is made up of two parts. **Pair** sounds like **pear**.

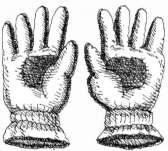

par·ents /pâr ənts/ *noun, plural*
1. A mother and a father.
2. A group of mothers, fathers, or mothers and fathers.

park /pärk/
1. *noun* An area of land with trees and playground that is used by people for rest and fun. **2.** *verb* To leave a car in a specific space or place.

part /pärt/ *noun*
1. A portion of the whole. **2.** A piece in a machine or device. **3.** A share of work. **4.** A role in a play or film. *Synonyms: portion, section, division*

par·ty /pär tē/ *noun*
1. A planned time when people get together to have a good time. **2.** A group of people who share a political belief.

paw /pô/ *noun*
The foot of an animal that has four feet and claws.

pear /pâr/ *noun*
A juicy, sweet fruit with a smooth skin. **Pear** sounds like **pair**.

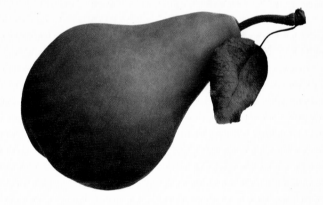

a	add	ô	order	ŧħ	this
ā	ace	o͞o	took	zh	vision
â	care	o͞o	pool		
ä	palm	u	up		
e	end	û	burn	ə	=
ē	equal	yo͞o	fuse	a	in *above*
i	it	oi	oil	e	in *sicken*
ī	ice	ou	pout	i	in *possible*
o	odd	ng	ring	o	in *melon*
ō	open	th	thin	u	in *circus*

pie /pī/ *noun*
A filled pastry that is baked in the oven.

pinch /pinch/ *verb*
To squeeze someone's skin between the thumb and index finger.

pitch /pich/
1. *verb* To throw or toss something. 2. *noun* The highness or lowness of a musical note.

plain /plān/ *adjective*
1. Easy to see or hear. 2. Easy to understand.
3. Simple; not fancy. **Plain** sounds like **plane.**

plan /plan/
1. *verb* To work out ahead of time how you will do something. 2. *noun* The idea for how you will do something. ▶*verb* **planning, planned**

plant /plant/
1. *noun* A living organism with a green color or pigment. 2. *verb* To put a plant or seed in the ground so that it will grow.

plas·tic /plas tik/ *noun*
A light but strong manufactured substance used to make many different things.

point /point/
1. *verb* To show where something is by using your index finger. 2. *noun* The sharp end of something.

poi·son /poi zən/ *noun*
A substance that can harm or kill if swallowed.

pop·corn /pop kôrn/ *noun*
A snack made from kernels of corn that are heated until they burst.

porch /pôrch/ *noun*
A structure with a roof on the side of a house.

print /print/ *verb*
1. To produce words or pictures on a page with a machine that uses ink. 2. To write using separate letters.

pro·gram /prō gram or prō grəm/
1. *noun* A television or radio show. 2. *noun* Instructions written in computer language.
3. *verb* To give a computer instructions to work in a certain way. ▶*verb* **programming, programmed**

punch /punch/
1. *noun* A drink of fruit juices, often mixed with soda. 2. *verb* To hit something or someone.

pur·ple /pûr pəl/ *noun*
The color made by mixing red and blue.

R r

rail·road /rāl rōd/ *noun*
1. A track of rails for a train. 2. A system of transportation using trains.

ranch /ranch/ *noun*
A large farm for cattle, sheep, or horses.
plural **ranches**

rang /rang/ *verb*
Past tense of **ring.** Made a clear, musical sound.

rath·er /rath ər/ *adverb*
1. Fairly or quite. **2.** More willing.

reach /rēch/ *verb*
To stretch out to something with your hand.

re·cess /rē ses or ri ses/ *noun*
A rest break from work or school.

re·plied /ri plīd/ *verb*
Past tense of **reply**. Gave an answer.

re·ply·ing /ri plī ing/ *verb*
Giving an answer.

ridge /rij/ *noun*
1. A narrow, raised strip on something.
2. A narrow chain of hills or mountains.

right /rīt/
1. *adjective* On the side opposite left. **2.** *adjective*
Correct. **3.** *adjective* Good, acceptable. **4.** *adverb*
Exactly. **5.** *adverb* Immediately. **Right** sounds
like **write**.

ring /ring/
1. *verb* To make or form a ring or circle.
2. *verb* To make a clear, musical sound.
3. *noun* A circle of metal worn on the finger
as jewelry. ▶ *verb* **ringing, rang, rung**

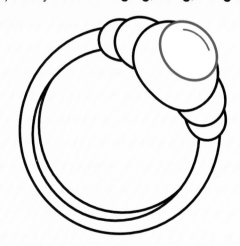

road /rōd/ *noun*
A smooth surface on which people and vehicles
travel. **Road** sounds like **rode** and **rowed**.

rode /rōd/ *verb*
Past tense of **ride**. Traveled on an animal or in a
vehicle. **Rode** sounds like **road** and **rowed**.

roof /roof or ruf/ *noun*
1. The top of a building or vehicle. **2.** The top
part of something.

rowed /rōd/ *verb*
Past tense of **row**. Used oars to move a boat
through water. **Rowed** sounds like
road and **rode**.

roy·al /roi əl/ *adjective*
Belonging to a king or queen or their family.

rude /rood/ *adjective*
Not polite.

rung /rung/ *noun*
Made a clear musical sound. Past tense of **ring**.
Rung sounds like **wrung**.

a	add	ô	order	th	this
ā	ace	o͝o	took	zh	vision
â	care	o͞o	pool		
ä	palm	u	up		
e	end	û	burn	ə	=
ē	equal	yo͞o	fuse	a	in *above*
i	it	oi	oil	e	in *sicken*
ī	ice	ou	pout	i	in *possible*
o	odd	ng	ring	o	in *melon*
ō	open	th	thin	u	in *circus*

S s

safe /sāf/
1. *adjective* Not in danger. 2. *adjective* Not risky.
3. *adjective* Careful. 4. *noun* A box used for locking up valuable papers and other items.

sail /sāl/
1. *noun* A large sheet of cloth that catches air and makes a boat move. 2. *verb* To travel in a boat or ship. **Sail** sounds like **sale**.

sale /sāl/ *noun*
1. The act of selling something. 2. A period of time when items are sold at a lower price. **Sale** sounds like **sail**.

sand·wich /sand wich/ *noun*
Two or more pieces of bread around a filling of cheese, meat, or some other food.

Word History

Sandwich owes its name to the man who invented this popular form of eating. The English Earl of Sandwich loved to play games and didn't like to leave the table for meals. He invented the sandwich so he could eat and play at the same time.

---

saw /sô/
1. *noun* A tool used for cutting wood. 2. *verb* To cut something with a saw.

scare /skâr/ *verb*
To frighten someone. ▶**scaring, scared**

sci·ence /sī əns/ *noun*
The study of nature and the physical world by testing and experimenting.

scis·sors /siz ərz/ *noun, plural*
A sharp tool with two blades used for cutting.

scout /skout/
1. *noun* Someone sent to find out and bring back information. 2. *verb* To look or search for something.

scram·bled /skram bəld/
1. *verb* Past tense of **scramble**. Mixed together.
2. *adjective* Mixed up.

scream /skrēm/ *verb*
To make a loud cry or sound.

scrib·ble /skrib əl/ *verb*
To write or draw carelessly.
▶**scribbling, scribbled**

scrub /skrub/ *verb*
To clean something by rubbing it hard.
▶**scrubbing, scrubbed**

sea·son /sē zən/
1. *noun* One of the four parts of the year. 2. *verb* To add flavor to food with herbs or spices.

sell /sel/ *verb*
To give something in exchange for money.
Sell sounds like **cell**.

sent /sent/ *verb*
Past tense of **send**. Made someone or something go somewhere. **Sent** sounds like **cent**.

Sep·tem·ber /sep tem bər/ *noun*
The ninth month of the year.

seven /sev ən/ *noun*
The number, written 7, that comes between six and eight.

shampoo /sham pōō/
1. *noun* A soapy liquid used for washing things.
2. *verb* To use shampoo.

shape /shāp/ *noun*
The form or outline of an object, such as a square or circle.

share /shâr/
1. *verb* To divide something between two or more people. 2. *noun* The portion one gets from sharing. ▶ *verb* **sharing, shared**

shark /shärk/ *noun*
A large, fierce fish with very sharp teeth.

shine /shīn/ *verb*
To give off a bright light.
▶ **shining, shined, shone**

shirt /shûrt/ *noun*
A piece of clothing that you wear on the top part of your body.

shook /shŏŏk/ *verb*
Past tense of **shake**. Moved quickly up and down.

should·n't /shŏŏd ənt/ *contraction*
A short form of *should not*.

should·'ve /shŏŏd əv/ *contraction*
A short form of *should have*.

shrink /shringk/ *verb*
1. To make smaller. 2. To draw back in fright.

shy /shī/ *adjective*
Bashful; timid.

side /sīd/ *noun*
1. An outer part of something that is not the front or the back. 2. The right or left part of the body. **Side** sounds like **sighed**.

side·walk /sīd wôk/ *noun*
A paved path beside a street.

sighed /sīd/ *verb*
Past tense of **sigh**. Breathed out deeply to show sadness or relief. **Sighed** sounds like **side**.

sil·ly /sil ē/ *adjective*
1. Not making sense. 2. Laughable.

a	add	ô	order	th	this
ā	ace	ŏŏ	took	zh	vision
â	care	ōō	pool		
ä	palm	u	up		
e	end	û	burn		
ē	equal	yōō	fuse	ə	=
i	it	oi	oil	a	in *above*
ī	ice	ou	pout	e	in *sicken*
o	odd	ng	ring	i	in *possible*
ō	open	th	thin	o	in *melon*
				u	in *circus*

sis·ter /sis tər/ *noun*
A girl or woman who has the same parents as another.

skin /skin/ *noun*
The outer layer of tissue on a human or an animal.

skunk /skungk/ *noun*
A black and white striped animal with a bushy tail.

sled /sled/ *noun*
A vehicle with runners used for traveling over snow.

slide /slīd/
1. *verb* To move smoothly over a surface. **2.** *noun* A playground ride with a smooth surface on which children can slide down. ▶ *verb* **sliding, slid**

slip /slip/ *verb*
To lose your balance or step, usually on a slippery surface. ▶ **slipping, slipped**

slow /slō/ *adjective*
1. Not fast. **2.** Behind the right time.

smart /smärt/ *adjective*
Clever and quick in thinking; intelligent.

smell /smel/
1. *verb* To sense an odor with your nose. **2.** *verb* To give off an odor. **3.** *noun* An odor or scent.

smooth /smōoth/ *adjective*
Even and flat; not rough.

snack /snak/ *noun*
A small, light meal.

snow·flakes /snō flāks/ *noun, plural*
Flakes of snow.

soft /soft/ *adjective*
1. Not hard. **2.** Smooth and gentle to touch.

soil /soil/
1. *noun* Dirt or earth where plants grow. **2.** *verb* To stain or make something dirty.

speak /spēk/ *verb*
To talk out loud. ▶ **speaking, spoke, spoken**

spell /spel/ *verb*
To write or say the letters of a word.

spend /spend/ *verb*
1. To use money to buy things. 2. To pass time.
▶ **spending, spent**

splash /splash/ *verb*
To throw a liquid.

spoil /spoil/ *verb*
To ruin something.

spring /spring/
1. *noun* The season between winter and summer when plants begin to grow. 2. *noun* A place where water comes from underground.
3. *noun* A coil of metal that returns to its original shape after being stretched or pushed down.
4. *verb* To jump suddenly. ▶ *verb* **springing, sprang, sprung**

square /skwâr/ *noun*
1. A shape with four equal sides. 2. An open area in a town or city.

stage /stāj/
1. *noun* An area where actors perform. 2. A level of development. 3. A stagecoach.

stairs /stârz/ *noun, plural*
Steps that go from one level to another.
Stairs sounds like **stares**.

star /stär/ *noun*
1. A ball of burning gases in space. 2. A shape with five or more points. 3. A person who is outstanding in some field.

stare /stâr/ *verb*
To look directly at someone or something.
▶ **staring, stared Stare** sounds like **stair**.

start /stärt/
1. *verb* To begin to do something.
2. *noun* The beginning.

star·tled /stär təld/ *verb*
Past tense of **startle**. Surprised or frightened someone.

step /step/
1. *noun* One of the flat surfaces on a stairway.
2. *verb* To move your feet forward, as in walking.
▶ *verb* **stepping, stepped**

stepped /stept/ *verb*
Past tense of **step**. Moved your feet, as in walking.

step·ping /step ing/ *verb*
Moving your feet, as in walking.

store /stôr/
1. *noun* A place where things are sold.
2. *verb* To put things away until they are needed.
▶ *verb* **storing, stored**

a	add	ô	order	ŧh	this
ā	ace	o͞o	took	zh	vision
â	care	o͞o	pool		
ä	palm	u	up		
e	end	û	burn	ə	=
ē	equal	yo͞o	fuse	a	in *above*
i	it	oi	oil	e	in *sicken*
ī	ice	ou	pout	i	in *possible*
o	odd	ng	ring	o	in *melon*
ō	open	th	thin	u	in *circus*

storm /stôrm/ *noun*
Heavy rain or snow that also has high winds.

straight /strāt/ *adjective*
1. Not bent or curved. **2.** Not curly.
3. Not crooked or stooping. **4.** Level.

stran·ger /strān jər/ *noun*
Someone you don't know.

straw /strô/ *noun*
1. Dried stalks of wheat or other
cereal plants. **2.** A thin, hollow
tube through which you can drink.

stretch /strech/ *verb*
1. To spread out your arms, legs, or body to full
length. **2.** To make something bigger or greater.

string /string/ *noun*
1. A thin cord or rope. **2.** A thin wire on a
musical instrument.

strong /strông/ *adjective*
1. Powerful; having a great force. **2.** Hard to
break. **3.** Having a sharp taste.

stud·ied /stud ēd/ *verb*
Past tense of **study**. Spent time learning a
subject.

stud·y /stud ē/ *verb*
1. To spend time learning a subject. **2.** To
examine something carefully.
▶studying, studied

stud·y·ing /stud ē ing/ *verb*
Spending time learning a subject.

sun·glass·es /sun glas iz/ *noun, plural*
Dark glasses that protect the eyes from the glare
of sunlight.

sun·set /sun set/ *noun*
The time of evening when the sun sinks in
the sky.

sun·shine /sun shīn/ *noun*
The light from the sun.

swam /swam/ *verb*
Past tense of **swim**. Moved through the water.

swamp /swämp/ *noun*
An area of ground that is wet and spongy;
a marsh.

sweet /swēt/
1. *adjective* Tasting like sugar or honey. **2.** *adjective*
Pleasant in taste, smell, or sound. **3.** *noun* A piece
of candy or other sweet-tasting food.

swim /swim/ *verb*
To move through the water by using your arms
and legs. ▶swimming, swam

swim·ming /swim ing/ *verb*
Moving through the water by using your arms
and legs.

teach·er /tēch ər/ *noun*
A person who shows someone how to do
something or helps them learn subjects in school.

tear /tēr/ *noun*
A drop of clear, salty liquid that comes from
your eyes.

thank /thangk/ *verb*
To tell someone you are grateful.

the·a·ter /thē ə tər/ *noun*
A place where movies or plays are shown.

their /thâr/ *adjective*
Belonging to them.

there's /thârz/ *contraction*
A short form of *there is*.

they're /thâr/ *contraction*
A short form of *they are*. **They're** sounds like
their and **there**.

thick /thik/ *adjective*
1. Not thin; very wide or deep. **2.** Not pouring
easily.

thing /thing/ *noun*
An object, idea, or event.

think /thingk/ *verb*
1. To use your mind to come up with ideas.
2. To have an idea or thought.
▶**thinking, thought**

thirst·y /thûr stē/ *adjective*
Needing to drink something.

throat /thrōt/ *noun*
The front of the neck.

thun·der /thun dər/
1. *noun* The loud, rumbling sound that comes
after a lightning flash. **2.** *verb* To make a sound
like thunder.

tie /tī/
1. *noun* A long piece of material that is knotted
and worn at the neck; necktie. **2.** *verb* To join
two pieces of string with a knot or bow.
▶*verb* **tying, tied**

tip·toe /tip tō/ *verb*
To walk very quietly as if
you were on the tips of
your toes.
▶**tiptoeing, tiptoed**

to·geth·er /tə geth ər/ *adverb*
1. With one another. **2.** In one group or place.

toy /toi/ *noun*
An object that children play with.

a	add	ô	order	th	this
ā	ace	o͞o	took	zh	vision
â	care	o͞o	pool		
ä	palm	u	up		
e	end	û	burn	ə	=
ē	equal	yo͞o	fuse	a	in *above*
i	it	oi	oil	e	in *sicken*
ī	ice	ou	pout	i	in *possible*
o	odd	ng	ring	o	in *melon*
ō	open	th	thin	u	in *circus*

trap /trap/
1. *noun* A special cage for catching animals.
2. *noun* Anything used to trick or catch someone.
3. *verb* To catch an animal or person with a trap.
▶ *verb* **trapping, trapped**

trash /trash/ *noun*
Things that have been thrown away; garbage.

tre·men·dous /tri men dəs/ *adjective*
1. Huge. 2. Very good.

trick /trik/ *verb* To fool someone.

trip /trip/
1. *verb* To stumble or fall. 2. *verb*
To cause someone to stumble.
3. *noun* A journey or a visit.
▶ *verb* **tripping, tripped**

tripped /tript/ *verb*
Past tense of **trip**. Stumbled or fell.

trip·ping /trip ing/ *verb*
Stumbling or falling.

truth /trooth/ *noun*
1. The real facts. 2. The quality of being honest.

turn /tûrn/
1. *verb* To change direction. 2. *verb* To spin.
3. *noun* A change in direction. 4. *verb* To change
appearance.

tur·tle /tûr təl/ *noun*
A reptile that can pull its
head, legs, and tail into
its hard shell for protection.

U u

up·stairs /up stârz/
1. *adverb* Up the stairs. 2. *noun* The upper floor or
floors of a house or building.

use /yooz/
1. *verb* To do a job with something. 2. *noun* The
act of using something. ▶ *verb* **using, used**

used /yoozd/ *verb*
Past tense of **use**. Did a job with something.

us·ing /yoo zing/ *verb*
Doing a job with something.

V v

vil·lage /vil ij/ *noun*
A small town.

voice /vois/ *noun*
1. The sound made when you speak or sing.
2. The power to speak and sing.

W w

wade /wād/ *verb*
1. To walk through water. 2. To move through
something slowly. ▶ **wading, waded**

wash /wosh or wôsh/
1. *verb* To clean with
soap and water.
2. *noun* Clothes that
need to be washed.

waste /wāst/
1. *verb* To spend or use foolishly.
2. *noun* Garbage; something not needed. ▶ *verb* **wasting, wasted**
Waste sounds like **waist**.

wast·ed /wāst əd/ *verb*
Past tense of **waste**. Spent or used foolishly.

wast·ing /wāst ing/ *verb*
Spending or using foolishly.

watch /woch/
1. *noun* A small clock worn on the wrist. 2. *verb* To look at something. 3. *verb* To be careful.

wa·ter /wô tər/
1. *noun* The liquid that falls as rain and fills oceans, rivers, and lakes. 2. *verb* To pour water on. ▶ *verb* **watering, watered**

weak /wēk/ *adjective*
Not strong; likely to break.
Weak sounds like **week**.

wear /wâr/ *verb*
To be dressed in something. ▶ *verb* **wearing, wore**

week /wēk/ *noun*
A period of seven days. **Week** sounds like **weak**.

weighed /wād/ *verb*
Past tense of **weigh**. Measured how heavy something is.

we'll /wēl/ *contraction*
A short form of *we will* or *we shall*.

were /wûr/ *verb*
Form of **to be** used with *we, you,* and *they* or plural nouns to show past tense, as in *We were happy*.

what's /wots or wuts/ *contraction*
A short form of *what is* or *what has*.

wild /wīld/
1. *adjective* Natural; not tame. 2. *noun* An area in its natural state.

wil·der·ness /wil dər nis/ *noun*
An area of wild land.

wind /wind/
1. *noun* Moving air. 2. /wīnd/ *verb* To wrap something around something else.

win·dow-shop·ping
/win dō shop ing/ *verb*
To look at things in store windows.

wink /wingk/ *verb*
To close one eye briefly as a friendly signal.

a	add	ô	order	th	this	
ā	ace	o͝o	took	zh	vision	
â	care	o͞o	pool			
ä	palm	u	up			
e	end	û	burn	ə	=	
ē	equal	yo͞o	fuse	a	in *above*	
i	it	oi	oil	e	in *sicken*	
ī	ice	ou	pout	i	in *possible*	
o	odd	ng	ring	o	in *melon*	
ō	open	th	thin	u	in *circus*	

won't /wōnt/ *contraction*
A short form of *will not*.

word /wûrd/ *noun*
A unit of spoken sounds or written letters that has a meaning.

wore /wôr/ *verb*
Past tense of **wear**. Was dressed in something.

work /wûrk/
1. *noun* The effort to get something done.
2. *verb* To get something done by using your energy. 3. *verb* To function properly.

world /wûrld/ *noun*
The earth.

worm /wûrm/ *noun*
A small animal with a long, soft body that lives in the soil.

wor·ried /wûr ēd/ *verb*
Past tense of **worry**. Felt uneasy about something.

wor·ry /wûr ē/
1. *verb* To be uneasy about something.
2. *noun* Nervousness. ▶ *verb* **worrying, worried**

wor·ry·ing /wûr ē ing/ *verb*
Being uneasy about something.

write /rīt/ 1. *verb* To put letters, words, or numbers on paper. 2. To be the author of a story or poem.
▶**writing, wrote, written Write** sounds like **right**.

yard /yärd/
1. *noun* A unit of length equal to 3 feet. 2. An area of ground next to a house or building.

yawn /yôn/ *verb*
To open your mouth wide and breathe in deeply.

year /yēr/ *noun*
The time it takes the Earth to make one circle around the sun; 365 days.

you're /yûr/ *contraction*
A short form of *you are*.

you've /yo͞ov/ *contraction*
A short form of *you have*.